My

Most Favorite

Dessert Company

Cookbook

Doris Schechter

PHOTOGRAPHS BY ZEVA OELBAUM

HarperCollins*Publishers*

My

Most Favorite

Dessert Company

Cookbook

Delicious Pareve Baking Recipes

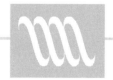

HarperCollins books may be purchased for educational, business, or sales promotional use. For information, please write: Special Markets Department, HarperCollins Publishers Inc., 10 East 53rd Street, New York, NY 10022.

FIRST EDITION

Book design by Claire Naylon Vaccaro
Printed on acid-free paper

Library of Congress Cataloging-in-Publication Data is available upon request.

ISBN 0-06-019786-2

06 07 08 09 ❖/RRD 10 9 8 7 6 5

This book is dedicated to my father, who instilled in me a deep respect and love for my heritage, to my mother, who taught me to never ever give up, and to my father-in-law, who believed in me and always said, "My money is on you, honey!"

Contents

Acknowledgments

Where do I begin to thank the innumerable people who over the years have participated in building My Most Favorite Dessert Company? The list is long. I will start in the most obvious place, with my family: my husband, Marvin, and my children, Philip, Stuart, Laura, Renée, and Dena, plus their respective husbands, wives, and children, twelve grandchildren in all at present count. In the very early days of the company, when we were in Great Neck, I relied on my children's help constantly. The girls stirred batter, baked, and boxed cakes. Laura, Renée, and Dena even delivered them. Laura's record of deliveries deserves special mention. It was flawless—not one ticket on all her runs—testimony to her skillfulness (to say nothing of her parking). My sons, and their many friends, made wonderful tasters, proving to me that with growing guys you can never, not ever, have enough cookies in the house!

Then, when the company moved to Madison Avenue in Manhattan, and it looked as if a much-needed renovation was never going to happen, Stuart galvanized a reconstruction crew. The Great Neck bakery was still very much in business at that time, and Dena, who was in her last year of high school, capably managed the store for me in my absence. It would never have happened without him. Not long after that, Renée, with her talented and sure hand, stepped in to run the bakery in Manhattan. She was the glue that held us together. Despite a busy family life, with two young daughters, Renée also very generously helped in testing the recipes for this book in her beautiful kitchen in Mamaroneck.

Which brings me to this book itself. I had always dreamed of doing a cookbook, but it was not until Carla Glasser called out of the blue one day that the dream came true. Carla introduced herself, explaining that she was a literary agent. She said she was convinced that there was a need for a collection of fine pareve recipes for the home cook and suggested putting together a proposal for such a book. Carla's instincts, as they have been all along over the course of this project, were right.

A book becomes real only when it is published, though, and my gratitude for that piece of the puzzle goes out to Susan Friedland, my editor, who accepted the manuscript and guided us over the course of its publication. It was a pleasure to learn from such a consummate professional.

To Zeva Oelbaum, a talented photographer, who was a delight to work with and a total team player, all my thanks.

To the many bakers I've known over the years, including Andre and Amilicar, who work in the bakery in Long Island City. Before a long day of baking, they were there to assist in the development of recipes for this project. Many thanks for *two* jobs well done.

To Scott, my son-in-law, who saw to it that business ran smoothly while I was involved on this project, heartfelt thanks.

To Evie Righter, who found my voice and in doing so became a dear friend. To many more happy times together.

Then, there is my dear friend Marsha, with whom I originally

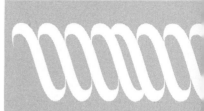

started the business. Our partnership ended, but our friendship survived. Bless you.

My sister Ruth, like my children, always seemed to be there at pivotal times. Her help was generous and frequently to the point. "Make it happen," she said.

To Rabbi Dale Polakoff, who as an assistant rabbi at Kehilath Jeshurun, on the Upper East Side in Manhattan in the mid-Eighties, was the driving force in convincing me to place my business under rabbinical supervision.

Finally, my thanks to my dear friend and mentor Ruth Gruber, whose life is exemplary in so many ways. "Dream dreams," she once told me. "Have visions. Let no obstacles stop you." Words cannot convey how much our friendship has meant.

Introduction

I was born the year Hitler marched into Austria. My parents were living in Vienna at the time. I never learned how my father obtained the visa that allowed him to leave Vienna for Italy not long after the Anschluss. He sent for my mother and me a short time later.

Italy became our adopted homeland. My father, a skilled linguist, worked as an interpreter for the United States Army. His duties included translating the speeches of Hermann Göring. We lived in Italy for almost five years, and it was there that my sister was born. In 1944, my family was among the 986 refugees invited by President Roosevelt to spend the duration of the war in the United States. We crossed the Atlantic in a perilous journey on an army transport ship called the *Henry Gibbons*. When we arrived in the United States we were taken to Oswego, New York, where we stayed for eighteen months. In 1946, my family started a brand-new life in the Bronx.

I went to school, just like other girls my age in the United States, but I felt incredibly different and longed to be a part of the world I

now found myself in. My given Austrian name was Dorrit. I changed it to Doris as a means to an end.

Our life was very family oriented, with Friday night dinners that my grandmother Leah always prepared. Unfailingly, Grandma would make her delicious apple cake, with its sweet thin crust and filling of apples with cinnamon. Grandma Leah was a very good cook, but her apple cake was far and away the best thing she made. Once a year, a friend of my mother's, Mrs. Monroe, made a special birthday cake for both me and my sister. I have never forgotten those cakes because nothing, not even a birthday cake, was taken for granted.

At eighteen, I married Marvin Schechter. Marvin's father, Itzak, was the most wonderful man. Every Sunday, Itzak would come to our house in Bayside, Queens, laden with boxes of pastries from a small Hungarian bakery not far from where he lived in Brooklyn. There were pounds of the most delicious diamond-shaped buttery sugar cookies and cakes. Marvin and I and our three small children would almost be waiting at the door for Itzak to arrive with his sweet surprises. This went on for years and continued when we moved, with a total of five children then, to King's Point, New York.

Then one day Itzak arrived empty-handed. No boxes, not one. "They retired to Florida," he explained. I begged Itzak to somehow track down the Hungarian owners and ask them for the recipe for their sugar cookies, which were the best I had ever tasted. The Hungarians were not to be found. Not only were Itzak's treats a thing of the past, but the bakery in Great Neck, close to our home, was only so-so.

By the time our youngest child, Dena, was in high school, it was time for me to find something to do outside of the home. Coincidentally, I was given a book on the cooking of Vienna. Anything associated with Vienna had always struck in me a very tender chord. Baking was a love of mine, and the first recipe I made from that book was a Viennese Linzertorte. I will never forget how incredible the aroma of the cinnamon, nutmeg, and raspberry jam was as it wafted through my house.

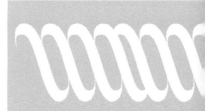

The finished tart was perfectly beautiful and tasted even better than it looked. The inklings of a career were starting to form. I had always baked for my family and now I baked more than ever before.

Because of my European heritage, I had always baked with butter. I was skeptical about pareve baking. A very good friend of mine was having a gala birthday party for her husband and we were invited. A party at Phyllis and Godfrey's house meant not only the most delicious food, but the most beautiful gardens and most perfect setting. Nothing was ever out of place. I wanted to give Godfrey something meaningful for his birthday and offered to do all the baking, with the exception of his birthday cake. His wife would bake the cake. Because they kept a kosher home and were serving a meat meal, that meant that whatever I baked would have to be pareve, meaning made without those foods designated dairy or meat by the rabbis and therefore acceptable to serve with both—neutral, in other words.

I wanted to prove to myself that pareve baking could be delicious and elegant. So I set about adapting recipes and testing them. I baked all kinds of cookies, meringues, Linzertortes—all of them pareve. My gift to Godfrey, those cookies and tarts, were incredibly well received and turned out to be the impetus for starting a baking business of my own. I had proven to myself that delicious pareve products were possible. My dear friend Marsha and I opened a small bakery in Great Neck in 1982, with carrot cake, apple cake, chocolate cakes, brownies, and cookies among our first offerings. My friend Toby asked what we were thinking of calling the company. Not waiting for me to answer, she allowed: "Doris, you're always saying, 'Oh, this is my *most* favorite . . .' "

"That's it," I said. "That's what we'll be called!"

Our products had a wonderful homemade look about them, and they flew out the door. Not for a second had we anticipated the reception our bakery received. Customers lined up waiting to get in. We could not make carrot cakes fast enough! Marsha and I wore every hat you can imagine—baker, deliverer, order taker. My children, my sister,

you name them, were called in to serve. One day Marsha told me that she had had enough and was going to go on a trip with her husband to China. I was devastated, but I understood. Baking is nothing if not strenuous.

Not one for giving up, I decided to forge on. All along I had quietly thought what fun it might be to have a My Most Favorite Dessert Company with a Manhattan address, where we could have a European-style coffeehouse, a little bit of Vienna uptown. In 1986, a space at 1165 Madison Avenue, between Eighty-fifth and Eighty-sixth Streets, came on the market. The space had to be totally rebuilt, but I loved it and signed on. But if ever there was a time when my hopes plummeted, it was then. Weeks went by, with a huge rent looming and not a stitch of work being done. Finally my son Stuart decided to take the matter into his own hands. With Stuart in charge, the job got done.

Once again the lines stretched out the door. There were reviews from Arthur Schwartz in the *Daily News* and Florence Fabricant in *The New York Times.* It was shortly afterward that my daughter Renée returned from California to New York to head up the bakery. My dream of a coffeehouse had evolved into a restaurant for breakfast and lunch. My past still played a part. We served pastas for lunch and lovely fresh salads as they are made in Italy. It was a challenging time, but day by day my dream was coming true.

On Madison Avenue we developed a devoted following. My Most Favorite Dessert Company was a restaurant and bakery that used only kosher ingredients, but for those members of the Jewish community who observed the dietary laws that was not enough. They inquired whether we might seek rabbinical supervision, because they could only patronize a business with certification by rabbis according to the Jewish dietary laws. I remember being encouraged by Rabbi Dale Polakoff at that time to take the next step.

With each of these inquiries, I was rereminded of the importance of my background. My father was an observant Jew. The traditions of my faith and my heritage colored every aspect of my life and my family's lives. I imagined how wonderful it would be to have a place where I accommodated Reform, Conservative, and Orthodox Jews, Christians, Buddhists—everyone and anyone—under one roof. I decided that My Most Favorite Dessert Company would go under certification—it was an easy decision, in fact—and we did in 1988. In accordance with the dietary laws, we now have two distinct product lines, pareve and dairy; we close early on Friday and remain closed until Saturday at sundown; we close for all the Jewish holidays.

As marvelous as our location on Madison Avenue was, the lease was drawing to an end in 1995. So, in 1996, we moved to our present location on Forty-fifth Street off the Avenue of the Americas. Our restaurant now serves breakfast, lunch, and dinner, and we have expanded to include a café for take-out foods as well.

I have been in business almost twenty years. In many ways I feel that I have come full circle in my life. I am the sum total of my experiences. I came to this country as a Jewish refugee from Italy, having been born in Vienna. I became an American and have loved being an American. I started baking, with the aromas of Vienna filling my head. I started a baking company where we make sugar cookies by the pound, and I think of dear Itzak. Grandma's Apple "Cake" is one of our most popular items. My love of American baking could not be more apparent: Brownies, chocolate cakes, and traditional fruit pies are on display as you walk into my restaurant. You can choose among them, and you can also choose between pareve and dairy. In reality, there *is* something for everyone.

Similarly, this cookbook is a compilation of my discoveries, my secrets, over the years. I am sharing them all. And just as you can choose between a pareve and a dairy cake in my restaurant, so can you use butter wherever margarine is called for in the recipes that follow.

Tradition affects every aspect of my life and connects me to my background. Baking pareve is a part of tradition. The fact that pareve baking can be delicious adds to, sweetens, the experience.

About the Recipes

My career in baking began in my home kitchen, so I think I know what works for other home cooks. These recipes are accessible; they require no specialized baking equipment apart from a standing electric mixer for combining cake batters, making frostings, and even for mixing pie crusts and other doughs. I feel that a mixer does the task, whether it is whipping, creaming, or blending, consistently and efficiently.

I call for unsalted margarine in the recipes in this book. I have always felt it to be the most successful substitute for butter. If you are serving a dairy meal, unsalted butter can be substituted for the margarine in any of the recipes that follow.

As for other ingredients, I cannot overemphasize the importance of using those that are of top quality. Use as many all-natural ingredients as possible. They impart the truest flavor and contribute the most to the whole. I have consciously avoided using hard-to-find, specialty ingredients. Any supermarket stocks the basics you will need, which include:

• All-purpose unbleached flour. It is not necessary to sift the flour beforehand unless called for in the recipe.

• Spices, such as cinnamon and nutmeg. Make sure they are full-flavored. The large economy-size jars now available in many supermarkets are tempting because they are considerably less expensive than the smaller jars. But spices lose flavor and become stale-tasting over time. I recommend buying them in small quantities and keeping them in a cool cabinet. If your spices are more than six months old, it is likely that they need to be replaced.

• Unsalted margarine, also sometimes labeled "unsalted (sweet)" on the package. This is the margarine that was used for all the recipes in this book. Be careful not to mistake salted margarine for the unsalted: I did that once—one does it only once!—and the recipe, a large batch of "buttercream," was inedible. For detailed information on this important ingredient, see About Margarine on page 13.

• Eggs. Extra-large fresh eggs were used throughout this book. They are not kosher if they contain blood spots. Before I add eggs to a recipe, I always break them, one at time, into a separate bowl to check them.

• Vanilla extract. Pure vanilla unquestionably has the best flavor, which is why I use it exclusively. Imitation vanilla flavoring is never a substitute.

• Citrus. Because I love what citrus adds to a recipe, whether it is in the form of juice or grated zest, I use only fresh citrus fruit. It is always a good idea to have a lemon and orange or two in the refrigerator.

• Chocolate. Two kinds of chocolate are called for in these pages: unsweetened and semisweet, or bittersweet. It should be pure and high-quality. We use a brand called Bloomer's. Any other good-quality chocolate, as long as it is kosher, can be used.

• Cocoa powder. It should be unsweetened and Dutch process.

A final note: As a matter of course, at the bakery and restaurant, each ingredient is checked for the correct rabbinical certification.

The Importance of an Oven Thermometer

Baking times are at best only indications of when a baked good is done. They provide a range, nothing more. And there is a reason for that. Ovens vary. The way an electric oven heats is different from how a gas oven works, and a convection air oven is different from the other two. The only way really to know how your oven heats is to test it with an oven thermometer. It is my experience that most ovens run hot. If that is the case, you can have your oven recalibrated, which is the best solution but not always practical, and even a recalibrated oven can still be several degrees off.

For the most reliable results, bake with the thermometer in the oven so you can see how hot your oven is. Use the thermometer reading to adjust the oven temperature, but know that even then it can take time for an oven to cool down or heat up. A good 10 minutes before the suggested finish time, start checking the recipe for doneness. That way you will not only have headed off the risk of overbaking, but also zeroed in on the approximate finish time, give or take a few minutes. In other words, do not wait to find out that the batch of cookies you've been waiting to take out of the oven is *over*done. How an oven performs can be challenging to a baker. Checking your baked goods removes much of the guesswork.

About
Margarine

Margarine was developed as a substitute for butter, and the impetus for its development came, surprisingly, from France and, specifically, from Napoleon III in 1869. Because of a scarcity of products made with animal fats at that time and shortages prior to the Franco-Prussian War in Europe, a synthetic edible fat was needed. A contest was held in France. In 1870, a French pharmacist-chemist won the contest by developing a product made with suet and milk. The product was not synthetic, but it was spreadable. The quest for an "economical butter" went on.

The process of hydrogenation, invented in 1905, succeeded in hardening animal fats or vegetable oils, thus making them solid at room temperature. A butter substitute had become a reality, thanks to the chemical reaction of a substance with molecular hydrogen. Margarine went into large-scale production. To make the product more closely resemble butter, manufacturers added preservatives, flavoring, such as salt, food coloring, and vitamins. According to some authorities, margarine did not really catch on in the United States until after 1950 as a result of the rationing of butter in the two world wars. Health considerations, the amount of saturated fat in one's diet, further whetted people's interest in margarine. The higher the amount of saturated fat in a product, the harder it is on one's cardiovascular system. The fact that margarine contains no cholesterol and less saturated fat than butter added to its attractiveness. So did its lower price.

That said, one might think that all margarine is created equal. One look at the number of choices in the margarine section of a refrigerated case in the supermarket, however, quickly dispels that notion. There are a bewildering number of choices: margarine, soft margarine, spread, oil spread, fat-free margarine, spray, butter-margarine blends. Some are made with animal products, and for the purposes of my bakery and this book I do not use them. Some are made with corn oil, cottonseed oil, soybean oil, or blends thereof. Margarine is sold in tubs, in sticks, in pound packages, in spray bottles.

Unsalted, sometimes simultaneously labeled "sweet," is the margarine that was used in the testing of the recipes in this book. It must be made with all-vegetable oils. Because not all of the margarines sold are kosher, and not all of the kosher margarines have the proper certification on the packaging, it is advisable to check the box. For measuring, it is easier to use margarine sold in stick form, as opposed to the pound blocks. If you are using margarine sold in block form, I would urge you to measure it with a baker's scale for accuracy. Fat-free or diet margarine, which contains, respectively, no fat or a reduced amount of fat and more water, is never a substitute for the recipes in this book. Store margarine in the refrigerator until you are ready to use it in a recipe. Do not leave it at room temperature, as you might butter, as margarine softens quickly. Because kosher margarine contains more unsaturated oils, it is considered soft margarine.

I have always believed that margarine, more than vegetable shortening or liquid vegetable oil, produces the best results in pareve baked

goods, closest to the flavor and texture of made-with-butter products. I have used such brands as Mother's and Migdal margarine over the years. If those brands are available to you, use them. If not, select another pareve margarine, store it properly, use it as directed, and see if you, too, aren't surprised by the excellence of the result.

Loaf
Cakes

Banana Walnut Loaf

Chocolate Chip Chocolate Loaf

Cranberry Orange Loaf

Pumpkin Walnut Loaf

Strawberry Tea Bread

Marble Loaf Cake

Carrot Cake

Apple Nut Raisin Cake

Honey Apple Cake

Glazed Orange Bundt Cake

Pineapple and Macadamia Nut Cake

Plum Upside-Down Cake

Zucchini Cake

Introduction

ℰ

Loaf cakes and cakes with fruit—apple, banana, carrot, and zucchini—as well as upside-down cakes are favorites both to bake and to eat. They are moist, sweet, easy to make, even easier to serve, *and* they keep. There's a big return on a small investment of time.

There is another reason why these cakes appeal. They are adaptable : They can be served for dessert, breakfast, or tea. Many can be toasted. Almost all of them freeze successfully, an important consideration when homemade baked goods are what you like to serve.

While all of the loaf cakes that follow are for every day, one, in particular, is a holiday cake : Honey Apple Cake (page 36), appropriate for Rosh Hashanah. For more Rosh Hashanah baking, see page 185 for Teiglach, or honey nuts.

The simple-to-put-together, eminently likable recipes in this chapter were among the first I ever made when I opened my bakery in Great Neck in 1982. Carrot Cake (page 32) and Apple Nut Raisin Cake (page 34) were my very first two products. They were popular then, and they still are, almost twenty years later.

Banana Walnut Loaf

MAKES ONE 9 × 5 × 3-INCH LOAF, 8 TO 10 SERVINGS

When we first opened our bakery in Great Neck in 1982, I made large banana walnut loaves, medium banana walnut loaves, and small banana walnut loaves—almost any size worked. I realized that banana bread, whatever the size, sells. The key to a really good finished loaf is a ripe banana—the riper the bananas, the better the flavor, the more delicious the bread.

1¾ cups all-purpose flour
1 teaspoon baking soda
1 teaspoon salt
¾ cup chopped walnuts
10 tablespoons (1 stick plus 2 tablespoons) unsalted margarine, melted and cooled
1 cup sugar
2 extra-large eggs
3 medium very ripe bananas, mashed to a puree
½ teaspoon pure vanilla extract

1. Preheat the oven to 350 degrees F. Grease the bottom and sides of a 9 × 5 × 3-inch loaf pan. Cut a strip of parchment paper to fit the bottom of the pan and line the pan with it. Do not grease the paper.

2. Sift together the flour, baking soda, and salt onto a sheet of wax paper. Add the walnuts and stir to combine them with the dry ingredients.

3. In the bowl of a standing electric mixer fitted with the paddle attachment, combine the melted margarine, sugar, and eggs; beat on medium speed until well combined.

4. Add the banana puree and beat until incorporated. Beat in the vanilla.

5. Reduce the speed to low and beat in the dry ingredients just until incorporated. Do not overbeat.

6. Spoon the batter into the prepared pan and smooth the top. Bake for 55 to 60 minutes until a cake tester inserted in the center comes out clean. Remove the pan to a wire rack to cool for 5 minutes, unmold the loaf, and remove the paper liner. Place the loaf right side up on the rack to cool completely. To store the loaf, wrap it in plastic wrap and store in the refrigerator for up to 1 week.

VARIATIONS

Banana Walnut Cake with Chocolate "Buttercream"

Grease and flour a 9-inch cake pan. Make the batter as directed in the recipe and spread it evenly in the prepared cake pan. Bake at 350 degrees F for 40 to 50 minutes until a cake tester inserted in the center comes out clean. Let stand on a wire rack for 10 minutes before unmolding onto the rack to cool completely. Make Chocolate "Buttercream" (pages 91 to 92). Slice the cake into 2 even layers and fill and frost them with the buttercream. Store, covered with a cake bell, in the refrigerator for up to 4 days.

TO FREEZE

Wrap the loaf in plastic wrap and place in a freezer bag. Freeze for up to 3 months.

TO DEFROST

On the day you plan to serve the loaf, remove it from the freezer, unwrap it completely, and let stand at room temperature until ready to serve.

Banana Walnut Muffins

Line a muffin pan with paper cup liners or grease the muffin cups. Make the batter as directed in the recipe. Fill each muffin cup about three-quarters full with batter. Bake at 350 degrees F for about 30 minutes, or until a cake tester inserted in the center of a muffin comes out clean. Remove the muffins and let cool on a wire rack. Makes 8 to 12 muffins, depending upon the size of the muffin pan.

Chocolate Chip Chocolate Loaf

I layer the chips in the center of this cake so they melt into a delicious chocolate layer. If you are serving dairy, you can split the cake horizontally into 2 even layers and fill the middle with whipped cream and strawberries. Fresh raspberries swirled into the whipped cream would be very good, too.

1 recipe Chocolate Cake batter (page 54)
¾ cup regular-size semisweet chocolate chips

1. Preheat the oven to 350 degrees F. Grease the bottom and sides of a 9 × 5 × 3-inch loaf pan. Line the bottom of the pan with parchment paper. Do not grease the paper.

2. Pour half the batter into the prepared loaf pan and smooth it into an even layer. Scatter the chocolate chips evenly over the batter. Scrape the remaining batter into the pan and level the top.

3. Bake the loaf for 1 hour, or until a cake tester inserted in the center comes out clean. Remove the pan to a wire rack and let cool for 5 minutes. Unmold the loaf and remove the paper liner. Invert the loaf right side up and let cool completely on the rack. To store, wrap it in plastic wrap and store in the refrigerator for up to 1 week.

MAKES ONE 9 × 5 × 3-INCH LOAF, 8 TO 10 SERVINGS

TO FREEZE
Wrap the loaf in plastic wrap and place it in a freezer bag. Freeze for up to 3 months.

TO DEFROST
On the day you plan to serve the loaf, remove it from the freezer, unwrap it completely, and let it stand at room temperature until ready to serve.

Cranberry Orange Loaf

MAKES ONE 9 × 5 × 3-INCH
LOAF, 8 TO 10 SERVINGS

Oranges are one of my favorite fruits. In this recipe I use freshly squeezed orange juice and you should do the same. I also like to add lots of freshly grated orange zest. For Thanksgiving I put a loaf of this cake at each end of the table and let guests help themselves. It enhances the holiday table. For me, this loaf, along with Pumpkin Walnut Loaf (page 26), is synonymous with Thanksgiving.

> 2 cups all-purpose flour
> 1½ teaspoons baking powder
> ½ teaspoon baking soda
> ½ teaspoon salt
> 4 tablespoons (½ stick) unsalted margarine, melted
>   and cooled
> 1 cup sugar
> 1 extra-large egg, beaten lightly
> ¾ cup fresh orange juice
> 1 tablespoon freshly grated orange zest
> 2 cups chopped picked-over and rinsed cranberries

I. Preheat the oven to 350 degrees F. Grease the bottom and sides of a 9 × 5 × 3-inch loaf pan. Cut a piece of parchment paper to

fit the bottom of the pan and line the pan with it. Do not grease the paper.

2. In a medium bowl, stir together the flour, baking powder, baking soda, and salt until combined.

3. In the bowl of a standing electric mixer fitted with the paddle attachment, combine the margarine, sugar, and egg. Blend on low speed for $1\frac{1}{2}$ to 2 minutes until very well combined.

4. With the machine still running on low speed, add the dry ingredients, a little at a time, alternating with the orange juice and ending with the juice, until blended. Mix in the orange zest. Using a rubber spatula, scrape down the sides of the bowl. Add the cranberries and mix them in by hand until well distributed.

5. Spoon the batter into the prepared pan and smooth the top. Bake in the middle of the oven for 50 minutes, or until a cake tester inserted in the middle of the loaf comes out clean. The top of the cake will be a rich golden color.

6. Remove the pan to a wire rack and let cool for 5 minutes. Unmold the loaf and remove the paper liner. (If the loaf does not unmold immediately, run a thin knife around the edge of the pan, then invert again, at which point the loaf should drop out.) Place right side up on the rack to cool completely. To store the loaf, wrap it in plastic wrap and store it in the refrigerator for up to 1 week.

TO FREEZE

Wrap the loaf in plastic wrap and place in a freezer bag. Freeze for up to 3 months.

TO DEFROST

On the day you plan to serve the loaf, remove it from the freezer, unwrap it completely, and let it stand at room temperature until ready to serve.

Pumpkin Walnut Loaf

MAKES ONE 9 × 5 × 3-INCH
LOAF, 8 TO 10 SERVINGS

When My Most Favorite Dessert Company opened on Madison Avenue in 1986, one of the first reviews we received was by Florence Fabricant in *The New York Times.* She loved our pumpkin bread, and that Thanksgiving season, thanks to her write-up, our pumpkin breads flew out the door.

This pumpkin loaf is rich-tasting and moist, thanks to an unusual ingredient: soy milk. I'd be surprised if anyone detects it. I can't. I like using Organic Vanilla Soy Milk by EdenSoy, which is available in some supermarkets and many health-food stores. It is pareve, as you will see from the label, and can be used as a substitute for milk.

2 cups sifted all-purpose flour

2 teaspoons baking powder

1 teaspoon ground cinnamon

1 teaspoon salt

1/2 teaspoon baking soda

1/2 teaspoon ground nutmeg

4 tablespoons (1/2 stick) unsalted margarine

1 cup sugar

2 extra-large eggs

1 cup pumpkin puree (Libby's Pumpkin—not
    pumpkin pie filling)

1/2 cup vanilla soy milk (see headnote)

1 cup chopped walnuts

1. Preheat the oven to 350 degrees F. Grease the bottom and sides of a 9 × 5 × 3-inch loaf pan. Cut a piece of parchment paper to fit the bottom of the pan and line the pan with it. Do not grease the paper.

2. In a medium bowl, stir together the flour, baking powder, cinnamon, salt, baking soda, and nutmeg.

3. In the bowl of a standing electric mixer fitted with the paddle attachment, cream the margarine and the sugar on medium speed until fluffy.

4. With the machine running, add the eggs, all at one time. Scrape down the sides of the bowl with a rubber spatula.

5. With the machine on medium speed, add the pumpkin and beat until combined.

6. Reduce the speed to low and add the dry ingredients, alternating with the soy milk, until blended. Scrape down the sides of the bowl and stir in the walnuts by hand.

7. Scrape the batter into the prepared pan and smooth the top. Bake for about 55 minutes, or until a cake tester inserted in the center comes out clean. Remove the pan to a wire rack and let cool for 5 minutes. Unmold the loaf and remove the paper liner. (If the loaf does not unmold immediately, run a thin knife around the edge of the pan and invert again, at which point the loaf should drop out.) Place it right side up on the rack to cool completely. To store the loaf, wrap it in plastic wrap and store it in the refrigerator for up to 1 week.

TO FREEZE

Wrap the loaf in plastic wrap and place in a freezer bag. Freeze for up to 3 months.

TO DEFROST

On the day you plan to serve the loaf, remove it from the freezer, unwrap it completely, and let it stand at room temperature until ready to serve.

Strawberry Tea Bread

The very first strawberry tea bread I ever made was with sour cream. Then I decided to use nondairy creamer for the sour cream, and I've been making it that way ever since. Although I am not in favor of using any synthetic products, sometimes it is unavoidable in order to serve a pareve dessert. Thank goodness for great strawberries! The fresh berries star in this quick bread.

This makes a lovely long loaf, perfect for a big gathering. Or do what I do, serve it whole, then freeze the part you don't eat. Cut the loaf into thin slices and serve them plain or with strawberry preserves for those who want a little more strawberry flavor. This bread is also good toasted.

3$\frac{1}{2}$ cups all-purpose flour
1 teaspoon baking powder
$\frac{1}{2}$ teaspoon ground cinnamon
$\frac{1}{2}$ teaspoon baking soda
$\frac{3}{4}$ teaspoon salt
12 tablespoons (1$\frac{1}{2}$ sticks) unsalted margarine
1$\frac{1}{2}$ cups sugar
4 extra-large eggs
$\frac{1}{2}$ cup nondairy creamer (see Note on page 29)
2 teaspoons pure vanilla extract
2 cups chopped hulled strawberries ($\frac{1}{2}$-inch pieces)
1 cup chopped walnuts

1. Preheat the oven to 350 degrees F. Grease the bottom and sides of a 13 × 4 × 4-inch loaf pan. Cut a piece of parchment paper to fit the bottom of the pan and line the pan with it. Do not grease the paper.

2. In a large bowl, place the flour, baking powder, cinnamon, baking soda, and salt and stir to combine.

3. In the bowl of a standing electric mixer fitted with the paddle attachment, cream the margarine and the sugar on medium speed until light and fluffy.

4. With the machine running, add the eggs, 1 at a time, and beat until well incorporated before adding the next egg. Scrape down the sides of the pan. Beat in the nondairy creamer and vanilla.

5. Add the strawberries to the combined dry ingredients, tossing them to coat. With the machine on low, gradually start adding the dry ingredients to the batter until incorporated. The batter will be thick and, when done, faintly tinted pink from the berries. Beat just long enough to crush some but not all of the berries. When needed, scrape down the sides of the bowl.

6. By hand, stir in the walnuts until evenly distributed.

7. Scrape the batter into the prepared pan and smooth the top. The batter will come about halfway up the sides of the pan. Bake the loaf on the middle rack of the oven for 1 hour and 20 to 25 minutes until golden brown on top and a cake tester inserted in the center comes out clean. (Don't worry if the bread should split on the top before it is done. It is not a sign of anything wrong. Quite to the contrary, it makes the loaf especially homemade-looking and pretty.) Remove the pan to a large wire rack to cool for 5 minutes, then carefully unmold the loaf and remove the paper liner. Place right side up on the rack and let cool completely. To store the loaf, wrap it in plastic wrap and store it in the refrigerator for up to 3 days. After that, the berries become too soft to be appealing.

TO FREEZE

Wrap the loaf in plastic wrap and place it in a freezer bag. Freeze for up to 3 months.

TO DEFROST

On the day you plan to serve the loaf, remove it from the freezer, unwrap it completely, and let it stand at room temperature until serving time.

Note: Nondairy creamer is widely available in pint containers and is sold in the refrigerator section or freezer section of almost any supermarket or food store. Once opened, it should be stored in the refrigerator, where it will keep for several weeks.

MAKES ONE 9 × 5 × 3-INCH
LOAF, 8 TO 10 SERVINGS

Marble
Loaf Cake

It is nice to be reminded that there are cakes like this one—old-fashioned and comforting. A slice of this is good with a glass of iced tea on a summer afternoon. If you feel the need to dress up the cake, bake it in a bundt pan, then drizzle it with Chocolate Glaze (page 102). Simply grease and flour the bundt pan—no need to line the bottom with paper, as we do with the loaf pan below. Be sure to let the bundt cake cool completely on a rack before unmolding and glazing it.

6 ounces semisweet chocolate, coarsely chopped
1 recipe Vanilla Cake batter (page 52)

1. Preheat the oven to 350 degrees F. Grease the bottom and sides of a 9 × 5 × 3-inch loaf pan. Cut a piece of parchment paper to fit the bottom of the pan and line the pan with it. Do not grease the paper.
2. In the top of a double boiler set over simmering water, melt the chocolate, stirring occasionally, until smooth and glossy. Remove the pan from the heat, but leave the top of the boiler over the water so that the chocolate remains warm and pourable.
3. Spoon the vanilla cake batter into the prepared pan and smooth the top with a rubber spatula. Pour the still-warm melted chocolate over the top of the cake and, with a metal spatula, swirl it through the

batter, making a marble pattern. Zigzag the spatula through the batter well, including into the corners of the pan. Really drag the spatula back and forth to ensure a beautiful design in the finished cake.

4. Bake the loaf for 1 hour, or until a cake tester inserted in the center comes out clean. Remove the pan to a wire rack and let cool for 5 minutes. Unmold the loaf and remove the paper liner. (If the loaf does not unmold immediately, run a thin knife around the edge of the pan, then invert it again, at which point the loaf should drop out.) Place the loaf right side up and let cool completely on the rack. To store the loaf, wrap it in plastic wrap and store it in the refrigerator for up to 1 week.

TO FREEZE

Wrap the loaf in plastic wrap and place it in a freezer bag. Freeze for up to 3 months.

TO DEFROST

On the day you plan to serve the loaf, remove it from the freezer, unwrap it completely, and let it stand at room temperature until serving time.

Carrot Cake

MAKES ONE 10-INCH TUBE
CAKE, 10 TO 12 SERVINGS

The very first time I ever tasted carrot cake was at my friend Susan's house, and I could not believe how delicious it was—so much so that it became the cake that put me into business! Little did I know when I first started making it at home, with my children and friends stirring up bowls of batter, where it all would lead.

During our first month or so in business, I even sold this cake as a "honey cake." I worried, but only a little. A week or so later, the customer I had sold it to came back into the store, and then I really worried. She said, "That was the best honey cake I've ever eaten. What's in it?"

"It must be the almonds," I said.

Thanks to my good friend Carla Glasser, I made a discovery about this cake. Carla wanted to serve it for a pareve meal, but she wanted it with frosting. (The traditional cream cheese frosting, which we offer at the restaurant, was out of the question.) Carla suggested Lemon "Buttercream" (page 92) for the cake, which turned out to be a wonderful match.

2 cups all-purpose flour
1 tablespoon ground cinnamon
2 teaspoons baking soda
1 teaspoon salt
3 extra-large eggs
2 cups granulated sugar
1½ cups canola oil

3 cups finely grated carrots (about 8 medium carrots, peeled—see A Little Piece of Advice)
1 cup very finely chopped (but not to powder) unblanched almonds
Confectioners' sugar, for sprinkling

1. Preheat the oven to 350 degrees F. Grease a 10-inch straight-sided tube pan with a removable bottom.
2. In a large bowl, stir together the flour, cinnamon, baking soda, and salt.
3. In the bowl of an electric mixer fitted with the paddle attachment, beat the eggs with the sugar on medium speed until lemon colored. Pour in the canola oil and beat until combined.
4. Add the dry ingredients to the egg mixture and beat on medium-low speed until combined. Stir in the carrots and the almonds until blended. Scrape the batter into the prepared pan, distributing it evenly and smoothing the top.
5. Bake on the middle rack of the oven for about 65 minutes, or until a skewer inserted in the center comes out clean. Remove the pan to a wire rack and let the cake cool for 15 to 20 minutes before unmolding it to cool completely.
6. When cool, serve the cake as is or dusted lightly with confectioners' sugar. This cake keeps well, wrapped in plastic wrap, in the refrigerator for up to 5 days. If you want to make it ahead and freeze it, you can do that up to 1 month in advance.

A Little Piece of Advice: I grate the carrots for this cake in a food processor fitted with the grating blade. If you don't have a food processor, you can use the side with the smallest holes on a hand-held box grater. As you can imagine, it will take you a lot longer.

Apple Nut Raisin Cake

MAKES ONE 10-INCH TUBE
CAKE, 10 TO 12 SERVINGS

Here is another simple-to-make cake that I have always loved because of its versatility. I have served it warm, for dessert; baked it into muffins, for breakfast; and had it just as is with coffee or tea. Like Carrot Cake (page 32), this was one of our first products and has always been a favorite—with our customers and my family. It is not a holiday cake per se, but it is comforting, especially in winter. In the restaurant we serve it with fresh whipped cream.

I always use McIntosh apples in this recipe and don't recommend substituting Granny Smith apples, despite their reputation of being good baking apples. They are too tart for my taste and don't have the right texture when baked. If you would like to use other apples, however, see page 119 for suggestions.

3 cups all-purpose flour
1 teaspoon baking soda
1 teaspoon ground cinnamon
1 teaspoon salt
3 extra-large eggs
2 cups granulated sugar
1 1/2 cups canola oil
5 medium McIntosh apples, peeled, cored, and coarsely
    chopped into 3/4-inch irregular pieces (3 cups chopped)
1 cup dark raisins
1 cup chopped walnuts
Confectioners' sugar, for sprinkling

1. Preheat the oven to 350 degrees F. Grease a 10-inch straight-sided tube pan with a removable bottom.

2. In a large bowl, stir together the flour, baking soda, cinnamon, and salt.

3. In the bowl of an electric mixer fitted with the paddle attachment, beat the eggs with the sugar on medium speed until lemon colored. Pour in the canola oil and beat until combined.

4. Add the dry ingredients to the egg mixture and beat on medium-low speed until combined. Add the chopped apples, raisins, and walnuts and stir to distribute them evenly. Spoon the batter into the prepared pan, smoothing the top evenly with the back of the spoon.

5. Bake the cake on the middle rack of the oven for 65 to 70 minutes until a skewer inserted in the middle of the round comes out clean. (The cake may crack on the top; this does not mean that it is over-baked.) Remove the pan to a wire rack and let the cake cool for 15 to 20 minutes before unmolding it.

6. Serve the cake warm, if desired. Or let it cool and serve it plain or dusted lightly with confectioners' sugar. Store the cake, wrapped well in plastic wrap, in the refrigerator for up to 5 days.

TO FREEZE

Wrap the cake in plastic wrap and place it in a freezer bag. Freeze for up to 1 month.

TO DEFROST

Unwrap the cake completely and let it stand at room temperature until thawed.

Honey Apple Cake

MAKES ONE 10-INCH TUBE CAKE, 10 TO 12 SERVINGS

One of the traditions of Rosh Hashanah, the Jewish New Year, includes pairing honey with apples, in the hope of sweetness in the coming year. The custom is to dip apple slices into honey. I decided to combine the apples and honey in one cake. The result is moist, subtly spiced, and deliciously sweet. I bake this in a round pan, symbolic of the hoped-for fullness in the new year. This cake can be served not only on Rosh Hashanah but over the course of the year as well.

3½ cups all-purpose flour
1¼ teaspoons baking soda
1¼ teaspoons baking powder
1¼ teaspoons ground cinnamon
½ teaspoon salt
¼ teaspoon grated nutmeg
1 cup plus 2 tablespoons sugar
2 tablespoons vegetable oil
2 extra-large eggs
1 cup honey
¾ cup brewed coffee, cooled
2 large McIntosh apples, peeled, cored, and finely chopped

1. Preheat the oven to 350 degrees F. Grease the bottom and sides of a 10-inch angel food cake pan. Cut a piece of parchment paper to fit the bottom and line the pan with it. Do not grease the paper.

2. Onto a large sheet of wax paper, sift together the flour, baking soda, baking powder, cinnamon, salt, and nutmeg.

3. In the bowl of a standing electric mixer fitted with the paddle attachment, combine the sugar, vegetable oil, and eggs. Beat on medium speed until combined.

4. Turn the machine off and add the honey. Beat on low speed until blended. Increase the speed to medium and beat for 30 seconds.

5. Turn off the machine again and add the dry ingredients, alternating with the coffee, until the batter is combined. (The batter will be loose.)

6. With a wooden spoon, stir in the chopped apples.

7. Pour the batter into the prepared pan and smooth the top. Bake for 1 hour 20 minutes, or until the cake is deep golden on top and a cake tester inserted in the center comes out clean. Remove the pan from the oven to a wire rack and let it stand for 5 minutes. Remove the sides of the pan and carefully remove the cake from the bottom. Let the cake stand right side up on a wire rack to cool. Store the cake, covered in plastic wrap, in the refrigerator for 1 week.

TO FREEZE

Make the cake as directed in the recipe, let it cool completely, then wrap it well in plastic wrap and place it in a large freezer bag. Freeze for up to several weeks.

TO DEFROST

Remove all the wrappings and let it stand at room temperature until ready to serve.

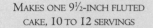

Glazed Orange Bundt Cake

MAKES ONE 9½-INCH FLUTED
CAKE, 10 TO 12 SERVINGS

When we first started our company in Great Neck, a friend of mine dropped by one day and said that she had just tasted a wonderful orange cake. Did we have such a cake? she wondered. We didn't, so I looked up a lot of recipes, started testing and experimenting, and came up with a cake that became one of our best-sellers. This pareve adaptation is a best-seller, too. What makes it so fantastic is its intense orange taste.

3½ cups all-purpose flour
2 teaspoons baking powder
⅛ teaspoon salt
½ pound (2 sticks) unsalted margarine
2 cups granulated sugar
6 extra-large eggs
½ cup vanilla soy milk (see headnote, page 26)
¼ cup fresh orange juice
2 teaspoons pure vanilla extract
Grated zest of 1 medium orange

GLAZE
½ cup fresh orange juice
¼ cup confectioners' sugar
2 tablespoons margarine (1 ounce)

1. Preheat the oven to 350 degrees F. Grease a 9½-inch fluted bundt pan.

2. Onto a piece of wax paper, sift together the flour, baking powder, and salt.

3. In the bowl of a standing electric mixer fitted with the paddle attachment, cream the margarine and the sugar on medium speed until fluffy and light. Beat in the eggs, 1 at a time, beating well after each addition.

4. In a bowl combine the soy milk, orange juice, and orange zest.

5. Reduce the mixer speed to low and add the dry ingredients, alternating with the soy-orange mixture, until the batter is combined. Scrape down the sides of the bowl with a rubber spatula.

6. Scrape the batter into the pan and smooth the top. Bake for about 55 minutes, or until a cake tester inserted in the center comes out clean. Invert the cake onto a wire rack and set the rack over a baking sheet or jelly-roll pan.

7. Make the glaze: In a small saucepan, combine the orange juice, confectioners' sugar, and margarine over medium heat, stirring until the margarine melts. Bring the mixture to a boil and let it boil gently for 5 to 8 minutes until it is syrupy and coats the spoon.

8. While the cake is still hot, brush it all over with the hot glaze, covering the top and sides generously. Let it stand at room temperature until the glaze sets. Store the cake for no more than 3 days under a cake bell at room temperature. Do not refrigerate it or the glaze will become sticky due to the humidity in the refrigerator.

Note: If you are making this cake in advance, freeze it before glazing it. Bake the cake as directed, let it cool, wrap it well in plastic wrap, and place it in a large freezer bag. Freeze for up to 3 months. On the day you plan to serve the cake, remove it from the freezer, unwrap it completely, and let it stand at room temperature until thawed. Then make the glaze. With a pastry brush, dab it on the cake, letting it soak in.

Pineapple and Macadamia Nut Cake

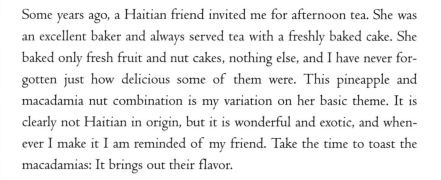

Some years ago, a Haitian friend invited me for afternoon tea. She was an excellent baker and always served tea with a freshly baked cake. She baked only fresh fruit and nut cakes, nothing else, and I have never forgotten just how delicious some of them were. This pineapple and macadamia nut combination is my variation on her basic theme. It is clearly not Haitian in origin, but it is wonderful and exotic, and whenever I make it I am reminded of my friend. Take the time to toast the macadamias: It brings out their flavor.

2½ cups macadamia nuts

2 cups all-purpose flour

1 teaspoon baking powder

½ pound (2 sticks) unsalted margarine

1 cup sugar

3 extra-large eggs

¼ cup pineapple juice (from canned pineapple)

1½ teaspoons freshly grated orange zest

1½ cups chopped canned pineapple

¼ cup rum, for brushing on the cake

1. Preheat the oven to 350 degrees F. Grease a 9½-inch fluted pan.

2. Spread the macadamia nuts on a baking pan and toast them in the oven, stirring once, until golden and fragrant. Remove the nuts, let them cool, and chop them.

3. Place the flour and the baking powder in a bowl and stir to combine.

4. In a standing electric mixer fitted with the paddle attachment, cream the margarine and the sugar on medium speed until fluffy and light. Scrape down the sides of the bowl with a rubber spatula.

5. With the machine running, add the eggs, all at one time, and beat until well combined.

6. Reduce the speed to medium-low and add the dry ingredients, a little at a time. Scrape down the sides of the bowl. Still on low speed, add the pineapple and the toasted macadamias and beat until well incorporated.

7. Spoon the batter into the prepared pan and level the top. (The batter will come up slightly past the halfway mark in the pan.) Bake on the middle rack of the oven for 45 minutes. When done, the cake will be golden brown and may have split on the top. Invert it immediately onto a wire rack. While the cake is still warm, brush it all over with the rum. Let the cake cool completely. Store leftovers, wrapped well in plastic wrap, in the refrigerator for 3 to 4 days.

Plum
Upside-Down Cake

I have never ever had any trouble getting upside-down cake to come out of the pan, although some people do. My advice to keep the cake from sticking is to unmold it while still hot—the sugar topping will not yet have hardened and the cake should slip right out. And if it doesn't, unmold the cake the best you can and reconstruct the top. It will still taste good.

In the fall substitute Italian prune plums for the red plums I use in the summer.

1 cup firmly packed dark brown sugar
4 tablespoons (½ stick) unsalted margarine, melted
5 large red plums, cut in half, pitted, and the halves
    cut into ¼-inch-thick round slices
1⅔ cups all-purpose flour
2 teaspoons baking powder
¼ teaspoon salt
5⅓ tablespoons unsalted margarine
⅔ cup granulated sugar
2 extra-large eggs
⅔ cup vanilla soy milk (see headnote, page 26)
1 teaspoon pure vanilla extract

1. Preheat the oven to 350 degrees F.
2. Spread the brown sugar evenly over the bottom of a 9-inch metal cake pan. Pour in the melted margarine and stir to dissolve the sugar. Spread the sugar mixture evenly over the bottom of the pan to cover it. Starting at the outside edge, place the larger plum slices in a circle around the edge of the pan. Then arrange a circle of plum slices in the middle of the pan, covering most of the sugar mixture. (There should be some space between the slices, but not too much.) Set the pan aside.
3. Into a bowl, sift together the flour, baking powder, and salt.
4. In the bowl of a standing electric mixer fitted with the paddle attachment, cream the margarine with the granulated sugar on medium speed until fluffy and light. Scrape down the sides of the bowl with a rubber spatula.
5. On medium speed, beat in the eggs, 1 at a time, beating well after each addition.
6. Combine the soy milk and the vanilla.
7. Add the dry ingredients, alternating with the soy milk mixture, to the batter and mix on medium speed until smooth.
8. Pour the batter evenly over the plum slices and the sugar mixture in the bottom of the cake pan. Carefully smooth the batter on the top, taking care not to disturb the pattern of the plum slices beneath. Bake the cake for 35 minutes, or until a cake tester inserted in the center of the cake (not into one of the plum slices) comes out clean. Transfer the pan to a wire rack and let it cool for about 5 minutes. Invert the cake, fruit side up, onto the wire rack. If the cake sticks, ease it gently out of the pan with the tip of a knife. Let the cake cool on the rack. This cake is at its best served freshly baked. Store leftovers, covered with plastic wrap, in the refrigerator for no more than 3 days.

V A R I A T I O N

Pineapple Upside-Down Cake

Make the brown-sugar topping as directed above, but use drained pineapple rings from a 16-ounce can in place of the plums. (You will have a few rings left over and may have to slice the inner pineapple ring into pieces in order to fashion the pattern in the center of the design.) Combine the batter and bake the cake exactly as directed.

Zucchini Cake

When I first started baking, I had never heard of a cake made with zucchini and, in all candor, the idea was not appealing. Then one day I decided to make one and discovered just how tasty it was. The cake has a moist crumb, with lots of cinnamon flavor, which makes it good to serve for dessert and tea, and breakfast, too. It keeps well.

MAKES ONE 10-INCH TUBE CAKE, 10 TO 12 SERVINGS

2 cups all-purpose flour
2 teaspoons baking soda
2 teaspoons ground cinnamon
1 teaspoon salt
1/4 teaspoon baking powder
2 cups sugar
1 cup vegetable oil, such as canola or corn oil
3 extra-large eggs
1 tablespoon pure vanilla extract
2 cups grated zucchini (2 small-to-medium zucchini)

1. Preheat the oven to 350 degrees F. Grease the bottom and sides of a 10-inch angel food cake pan with a removable bottom. Cut a piece of parchment paper to fit the bottom of the pan and line the pan with it. Do not grease the paper.

2. In a large bowl, stir together the flour, baking soda, cinnamon, salt, and baking powder.

3. In the bowl of a standing electric mixer fitted with the paddle attachment, blend the sugar and the vegetable oil on medium speed until well combined. Add the eggs, all at one time, and beat for a minute or two until light. Beat in the vanilla.

4. Reduce the mixer speed to low and add the dry ingredients, a little at a time, until incorporated. Mix in the grated zucchini on low speed.

5. Pour the batter into the prepared pan. Bake for 50 minutes, or until a cake tester inserted in the center comes out clean. Remove the cake to a wire rack and let it cool for 5 minutes. Lift the cake out of the pan. Invert it carefully, turn it right side up, and let it cool completely on the rack. To store the cake, wrap it in plastic wrap and store it in the refrigerator for up to 1 week.

Layer Cakes
and Specialty
Cakes

FOUNDATION CAKES

Vanilla Cake

Chocolate Cake

Génoise

Almond Génoise Half-Sheet Cake

LAYER CAKES

Orange Cake with Orange Buttercream

Génoise with Lemon Buttercream

Mrs. Monroe's Chocolate Cake

Almond Génoise with Chocolate
Buttercream

Shadow Cake

Vanilla Cake with Ganache Filling and
Chocolate Glaze

SPECIALTY CAKES

Doris's Blackout Cake

Dr. Paul's Rich Chocolate Cake

Doris's Sacher Torte

Dumont Torte

Viennese Linzertorte

FILLINGS, FROSTINGS, AND DECORATIONS

Vanilla "Buttercream"

Orange-Scented Sugar Syrup

Chocolate Pudding

Chocolate Mousse

Dr. Paul's "Ganache"

Chocolate Glaze

Meringue Mushrooms

Introduction

In 1985, I started to develop pareve layer cakes, and the endeavor, not surprisingly, took time. After quite a few tries, I had finished one cake, satisfied that the génoise layer I had just made with margarine was as light as a classic génoise and the "buttercream" that spread so beautifully was as tasty and smooth as the traditional one made with butter. I had proven to myself, the harshest critic of all, that a classic cake, plus the frosting and filling, could not only be made pareve but be delicious as well. I can't tell you what a thrill it was.

Now the fun began. I wanted to offer European-style cakes, typically American-style cakes, and tortes. I developed them, and they sold. Those are the cakes you will find in the following pages. The words "elegant" and "fancy" describe them best. Many of them are made with chocolate and/or nuts—two ingredients I love.

Some of the recipes, Shadow Cake, Dr. Paul's Rich Chocolate Cake, and my Sacher Torte, are involved and require making a cake, a filling, and a separate frosting and/or glaze. While all that may strike you as a daunting job, if you do it in stages it won't be hard. Specialty cakes are meant to be special, and these are.

In this chapter, then, are all the components for making a cake, from the foundation layers—basic vanilla, chocolate, or génoise cakes—to the fillings and frostings, including my signature garnish, fanciful meringue mushrooms. The assembled cakes are my favorites. Use the components to create delectable favorites of your own.

Foundation Cakes

The four cakes that follow—vanilla, chocolate, génoise, and almond génoise sheet cake—are the mainstays of my cake repertoire. In the section Layer Cakes and Specialty Cakes in this chapter, you will see how I mix and match the foundation cakes with the fillings and frostings. Some of the combinations are simple, others elaborate. Develop your own favorite combinations from the recipes. The basics are all here, including an extra or two, like my signature meringue mushrooms. Making cakes, whether simple or special, has always been what I've loved best. It all starts with a cake.

Vanilla Cake

This makes an excellent foundation cake and, without too much effort, a wonderful "old-fashioned" birthday cake as well. It can also be turned, Cinderella-like, into exceptional special-occasion desserts, like Shadow Cake (page 68) or Vanilla Cake with Ganache Filling and Chocolate Glaze (page 71). Its success comes as a result of its adaptability, and I showcase it in just that way, as you will see in this chapter. You can even serve it plain, with Fresh Strawberry Sauce (page 234) as the only accompaniment.

> 1³/₄ cups all-purpose flour
> 1 teaspoon baking powder
> Pinch of salt
> 1 teaspoon pure vanilla extract
> ¹/₄ cup vanilla soy milk (see headnote, page 26)
> 8 tablespoons (1 stick) unsalted margarine
> 1 cup sugar
> 3 extra-large eggs

1. Preheat the oven to 350 degrees F. Grease the bottom and sides of one 9-inch cake pan. Cut out a round of parchment paper to line the bottom of the pan and line the pan with it. Do not grease the paper.
2. Onto a large sheet of wax paper, sift together the flour, baking powder, and salt.

3. Stir the vanilla into the soy milk.

4. In the bowl of a standing electric mixer fitted with the paddle attachment, cream the margarine and sugar on medium speed until light. Scrape down the sides of the bowl with a rubber spatula.

5. Add the eggs, 1 at a time, beating well after each addition.

6. Reduce the mixer speed to low and start adding the dry ingredients, alternating with the soy milk mixture, beating until the batter is smooth and the ingredients have been fully incorporated.

7. Spoon the batter into the prepared pan and smooth the top. Bake for 40 minutes, or until a cake tester inserted in the center comes out clean. Remove the pan from the oven and let it stand for 5 minutes. Unmold, remove the paper liner, and place the cake right side up on a wire rack to cool.

AN OLD-FASHIONED BIRTHDAY CAKE

What is an old-fashioned birthday cake? To me, it is the best kind: simple white (vanilla) cake with chocolate "buttercream" plus, of course, rosettes, an inscription, and candles on top. I can help you with the cake (opposite) and a selection of "buttercreams" (pages 90 and forward). The decorating you must work on yourself.

TO FREEZE

Wrap the cooled layer securely in plastic wrap, then place it in a freezer bag and freeze for 1 month.

TO DEFROST

Unwrap it completely and let it stand at room temperature. Trim and frost as directed in the recipe.

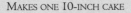

Chocolate Cake

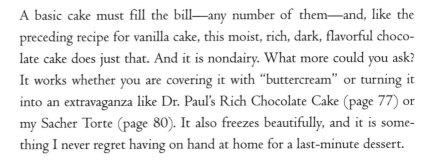

MAKES ONE 10-INCH CAKE

A basic cake must fill the bill—any number of them—and, like the preceding recipe for vanilla cake, this moist, rich, dark, flavorful chocolate cake does just that. And it is nondairy. What more could you ask? It works whether you are covering it with "buttercream" or turning it into an extravaganza like Dr. Paul's Rich Chocolate Cake (page 77) or my Sacher Torte (page 80). It also freezes beautifully, and it is something I never regret having on hand at home for a last-minute dessert.

1½ cups all-purpose flour
½ cup unsweetened cocoa powder
1 teaspoon baking soda
¾ teaspoon salt
¼ teaspoon baking powder
2 teaspoons pure vanilla extract
1 cup strong, freshly brewed coffee, cooled
8 tablespoons (1 stick) unsalted margarine
1½ cups sugar
4 extra-large eggs

I. Preheat the oven to 350 degrees F. Grease the bottom and sides of a 10-inch cake pan. Cut out a round of parchment paper to fit the bottom and line the pan with it. Do not grease the paper.

2. Onto a sheet of wax paper, sift together the flour, cocoa powder, baking soda, salt, and baking powder.

3. Stir the vanilla into the cooled coffee.

4. In the bowl of a standing electric mixer fitted with the paddle attachment, cream the margarine with the sugar on medium speed until lightened and fluffy. Scrape down the sides of the bowl with a rubber spatula.

5. With the machine running, add the eggs, all at one time, and beat until incorporated.

6. Reduce the mixer speed to low, and start adding the dry ingredients, alternating with the coffee mixture, beating until the batter is smooth and the ingredients have been fully incorporated.

7. Pour the batter into the prepared cake pan and smooth the top with the spatula. Bake for 45 minutes, or until a cake tester inserted in the center comes out clean. Remove the pan from the oven and let it stand for 5 minutes. Unmold the cake, remove the paper liner, and place the cake right side up on a wire rack to cool.

TO FREEZE
Wrap the cooled layer securely in plastic wrap, place it in a freezer bag, and freeze for 1 month.

TO DEFROST
Unwrap it completely and let it stand at room temperature. Trim and frost as directed in the recipe.

Génoise

Makes one 10-inch cake,
about 1¾ inches high

Some people say that it is not possible to make a good génoise without butter. I don't agree and prove it with this génoise made with margarine. You will need a candy thermometer, and it is important to follow the directions carefully: Allow the batter to beat until it is tripled in volume, which will seem like a long time. There is the temptation to rush it, but don't because that will affect the outcome. If you are looking for a light and elegant spongelike cake, this is it.

Génoise lends itself to a "buttercream" filling and frosting. A lovely example of just that combination, using lemon buttercream, appears on page 61.

> 5 whole extra-large eggs
> 1 extra-large egg white
> ¾ cup sugar
> ½ teaspoon salt
> 1½ cups all-purpose flour
> 4 tablespoons (½ stick) unsalted margarine, melted
>   and cooled

I. Preheat the oven to 375 degrees F. Grease the bottom and sides of a 10-inch cake pan. Cut out a round of parchment paper to fit the bottom and line the pan with it. Do not grease the paper.

2. In a medium saucepan, combine the whole eggs, egg white, sugar, and salt. Place the pan over medium-low heat and cook, stirring, until the sugar dissolves and the mixture reaches 110 degrees F on a candy thermometer. (The mixture will be barely warm when tested on the wrist.)

3. Transfer the warmed egg mixture to the bowl of a standing electric mixer fitted with the whisk attachment, and beat it on high speed for a full 5 minutes until thick, pale in color, and triple in volume. When ready, the mixture will stand in peaks when the whisk attachment is removed and swept through it.

4. Remove the bowl from the mixer and gradually fold in the flour, a little at a time, until incorporated. Fold in the cooled margarine.

5. Scrape the batter into the prepared cake pan and smooth the top with the spatula. Bake the cake for 25 to 30 minutes until lightly golden on the top. Remove the pan from the oven and let it stand for 5 minutes. Unmold the cake, remove the paper liner, and let the cake stand right side up on a wire rack to cool completely.

TO FREEZE

Wrap the cake securely in plastic wrap, place it in a freezer bag, and freeze for up to 2 weeks.

TO DEFROST

Unwrap it and let it stand at room temperature. Trim and frost as directed in the recipe.

Almond Génoise
Half-Sheet Cake

Cakes with nuts are among my favorites. Be sure to grind the almonds very fine—almost, but not quite, to powder. Because this is so light, it makes a fantastic layer cake, especially when filled with chocolate "buttercream" and covered with lots of toasted almonds, as directed on page 66.

If you are considering baking this ahead of time and storing it at room temperature, do so only 1 day in advance of finishing and be sure to wrap the pan well with plastic wrap, otherwise the cake dries out. The sheet can also be frozen. For directions, see the opposite page.

5 whole extra-large eggs
1 extra-large egg white
¾ cup sugar
½ teaspoon salt
¾ cup all-purpose flour
¾ cup very finely ground unblanched almonds
4 tablespoons (½ stick) unsalted margarine, melted
    and cooled

1. Preheat the oven to 375 degrees F. Grease the bottom and sides of a 17 × 12-inch half-sheet pan. Line the bottom with parchment paper, but do not grease the paper.

2. Make the génoise batter following the directions in Steps 2 and 3 on pages 56–57.

3. Remove the bowl from the mixer and gradually fold in the flour, a little at a time, until incorporated. Fold in the almonds in the same manner. Fold in the cooled margarine until incorporated.

4. Spread the batter in an even layer on the prepared sheet pan. Be sure it reaches into the corners of the pan. Bake for about 8 minutes, or until lightly browned on the top. Remove the pan from the oven and let the sheet cake cool in the pan.

TO FREEZE

You will need a large freezer. Let the cake cool completely in the pan, then wrap it in plastic wrap and slide the pan into the freezer for up to 1 week.

TO DEFROST

Unwrap it and let it stand at room temperature. Trim and frost as directed in the recipe.

Layer Cakes

Orange Cake with Orange Buttercream

MAKES ONE 2-LAYER 9-INCH
CAKE, 12 TO 14 SERVINGS

As I said earlier, orange is one of my favorite flavors, which makes this cake, with fresh orange juice in both the batter and the frosting, hard to resist. I particularly like to serve it in the winter because it reminds me of sunnier times (not to mention that winter is the best season for buying oranges).

If piping "buttercream" rosettes is not for you, garnish the top of the cake with small circles or mounds of buttercream, then lay long-stemmed strawberries between the mounds.

1 recipe Glazed Orange Bundt Cake batter (page 38)
About ⅓ cup Orange-Scented Sugar Syrup, or more
as desired (optional, page 94)
1 recipe Orange "Buttercream" (page 93)

1. Preheat the oven to 350 degrees F. Grease the bottom and sides of two 9-inch cake pans. Cut a round of parchment paper to line each pan and fit the rounds inside the pans. Do not grease the paper.

2. Divide the cake batter evenly between the 2 prepared pans and smooth the top. Bake the layers for 45 minutes, or until a cake tester inserted in the center comes out clean. Transfer the pans to cake racks and let cool for 5 minutes. Unmold the layers, remove the paper liners, place the cakes right side up on the racks, and let cool completely.

3. Stack the cooled layers on top of each other. With a long-bladed serrated knife, trim the edges of any hardened crust all the way around.

4. Place one of the layers on a cake stand or cake plate. Brush the top lightly with some of the orange sugar syrup, if desired. Spread orange buttercream evenly over the top of the layer.

5. Brush the top of the remaining cake layer with sugar syrup, if using, then invert it onto the buttercream. Brush the top with the remaining sugar syrup.

6. With a metal spatula, frost the sides and top of the cake with the remaining buttercream, reserving some of it for making rosettes, if desired. To make rosettes, transfer the remaining buttercream to a small pastry bag fitted with a star tip. Pipe small rosettes around the top rim of the cake. Serve. Store leftover cake, covered with a cake bell or lightly with plastic wrap, in the refrigerator for up to 4 days.

Génoise with Lemon Buttercream

I love this cake because it is the essence of lemon. Garnish it with fresh raspberries or blueberries, or serve it with raspberry sauce, if desired.

> 1 Génoise (page 56), cooled
> About ⅓ cup Lemon Sugar Syrup, or more as desired
> (optional, page 95)
> 1 recipe Lemon "Buttercream" (page 92)

1. With a long-bladed serrated knife, horizontally slice off the crown of the cake to make a level, even layer. With the knife, slice the génoise into 2 equal layers. Place the layers on top of each other and trim any hard edges all the way around. Discard the trimmings.

2. Place one of the layers on a cake stand or cake plate. Brush the top lightly with some of the lemon sugar syrup, if desired. Spread lemon buttercream evenly over the top of the layer to serve as filling.

3. Brush the top of the remaining layer of génoise with sugar syrup, if using, then invert it onto the buttercream. Brush the top of the génoise with sugar syrup.

4. With a metal spatula, frost the sides and top of the cake with the remaining buttercream, reserving some of it for making rosettes, if desired. To make rosettes, transfer the remaining buttercream to a small pastry bag fitted with a small star tip. Pipe rosettes around the rim of the cake. Serve. Store leftover cake, covered with a cake bell or lightly with plastic wrap, in the refrigerator for 3 days.

Mrs. Monroe's Chocolate Cake

MAKES ONE 2-LAYER 8-INCH
CAKE, 10 TO 12 SERVINGS

While I prefer to use margarine when making pareve desserts, I know other people, including my editor Susan Friedland, prefer to use oil. Here, then, is a cake, made with vegetable oil, that has a great chocolate frosting containing margarine. Something for everyone! I call it Mrs. Monroe's cake because it comes closest to the birthday cakes Mrs. Monroe, my mother's dear friend, used to bake for my sister and me when we were growing up. And, yes, it makes a wonderful special-occasion cake, especially if you decorate the top with a border of shells.

CAKE

2 cups granulated sugar

1¾ cups all-purpose flour

1½ teaspoons baking powder

1½ teaspoons baking soda

1 teaspoon salt

2 extra-large eggs

1 cup vanilla soy milk (see headnote, page 26)

½ cup vegetable oil

2 teaspoons pure vanilla extract

1 cup boiling water

FROSTING

8 tablespoons (1 stick) unsalted margarine, melted
    and cooled

⅔ cup unsweetened cocoa powder, sifted

3 cups confectioners' sugar, sifted

⅓ cup vanilla soy milk, or more, as needed

1 teaspoon pure vanilla extract

1. Preheat the oven to 350 degrees F. Grease and flour two 8-inch cake pans.

2. In the bowl of a standing electric mixer fitted with the paddle attachment, stir together the sugar, flour, baking powder, baking soda, and salt until combined. Add the eggs, soy milk, vegetable oil, and vanilla and beat on medium speed for 2 minutes. Stir in the boiling water. (The batter will be thin.)

3. Divide the batter equally between the 2 prepared cake pans and bake for 30 to 35 minutes until a cake tester inserted in the center of the layers comes out clean. Transfer the pans to wire racks and let cool for 10 minutes. Unmold the layers, invert right side up, and let cool completely.

4. Make the frosting: In the bowl of an electric mixer fitted with the paddle attachment, combine the melted margarine and the cocoa until blended. Add the confectioners' sugar a little at a time, alternating with the soy milk and adding more soy milk, if necessary, until the frosting has good spreading consistency. Stir in the vanilla.

5. Place one of the layers on a cake stand or cake plate and spread the top evenly with frosting. Top with the remaining cake. Frost the top and sides of the cake. Serve. Store leftover cake, covered with a cake bell or lightly with plastic wrap, in the refrigerator for up to 3 days.

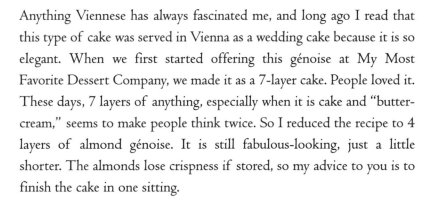

Almond Génoise with Chocolate Buttercream

Makes one 12 × 4-inch 4-
layer loaf, 10 to 12 servings

Anything Viennese has always fascinated me, and long ago I read that this type of cake was served in Vienna as a wedding cake because it is so elegant. When we first started offering this génoise at My Most Favorite Dessert Company, we made it as a 7-layer cake. People loved it. These days, 7 layers of anything, especially when it is cake and "buttercream," seems to make people think twice. So I reduced the recipe to 4 layers of almond génoise. It is still fabulous-looking, just a little shorter. The almonds lose crispness if stored, so my advice to you is to finish the cake in one sitting.

> **1 Almond Génoise Half-Sheet Cake (page 58), cooled**
> **1 cup sliced almonds**
> **1 recipe Chocolate "Buttercream" (page 91)**

1. After removing the half-sheet cake from the oven to cool, leave the oven on. Spread the sliced almonds in an even layer on a small baking sheet. Toast the almonds, turning them once, for 5 to 10 minutes until golden. Remove from the oven and let cool on the baking sheet.

2. Invert the half-sheet cake onto the work surface and remove the parchment paper. Trim the edges on both of the short ends of any

hardened crust, removing as much as ½ inch on each end. (Have a few bites: Even unfrosted, the génoise is wonderful.)

3. Using a ruler to make the edges straight, cut the cake crosswise into 4 even 4-inch-wide strips, each 12 inches long.

4. Place 1 of the cake layers on a long cake tray and spread the surface with chocolate buttercream. Top with another cake layer, spread it with buttercream, then proceed to make 2 more layers in the same manner, using the same amount of buttercream, more or less, between the layers.

5. Frost the sides and top of the cake with buttercream. When the surface is entirely covered in a smooth, even layer, press the toasted almonds over the cake, covering it completely. Serve. The cake will keep, covered with a cake bell or lightly with plastic wrap, in the refrigerator for 2 to 3 days, but the almonds will lose their delicious crunchiness.

Shadow Cake

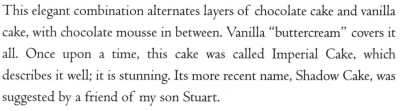

Makes one 3-layer 9-inch
cake, 12 to 16 servings

This elegant combination alternates layers of chocolate cake and vanilla cake, with chocolate mousse in between. Vanilla "buttercream" covers it all. Once upon a time, this cake was called Imperial Cake, which describes it well; it is stunning. Its more recent name, Shadow Cake, was suggested by a friend of my son Stuart.

This cake is ideal to serve when you have vanilla cake lovers and chocolate cake lovers at the same birthday table. It works for everyone.

> 1 recipe Chocolate Cake batter (page 54)
> About 1 cup Orange-Scented Sugar Syrup (optional, page 94)
> 1 recipe Chocolate Mousse (page 98)
> 1 Vanilla Cake (page 52), cooled, trimmed, and halved horizontally (see Note on page 70)
> 1 recipe Vanilla "Buttercream" (page 90)
> Chocolate Glaze (page 102), warmed, for piping the floral design on the cake

1. Preheat the oven to 350 degrees F. Grease the bottom and sides of two 9-inch cake pans. Cut a round of parchment paper to line the bottom of each pan and line each pan with a round. Do not grease the paper.
2. Divide the chocolate batter evenly between the 2 prepared cake pans and bake for 25 to 35 minutes until a cake tester inserted in the center comes out clean. Remove the pans from the oven and let stand

for 5 minutes. Unmold, remove the paper liners, and invert right side up to cool completely.

3. Stack the cooled layers on top of each other. With a long-bladed serrated knife, trim the edges of any hardened crust all the way around. Place the trimmings in a plastic bag and freeze. (Use the trimmings for the crumb covering on Doris's Blackout Cake on page 75.)

4. Place one of the chocolate layers on a cake stand or cake plate. Brush the top with some of the orange sugar syrup, if desired.

5. Measure about 1¼ cups chocolate mousse. With a spatula spread it over the chocolate layer.

6. Brush the vanilla cake layer with orange sugar syrup, if using, and invert it onto the chocolate mousse. Brush the top with sugar syrup.

7. Measure another 1¼ cups chocolate mousse and spread it over the vanilla cake layer.

8. Brush the remaining chocolate cake layer with sugar syrup and invert it onto the mousse. Brush with sugar syrup.

9. With a clean spatula, frost the top and sides of the cake with the vanilla buttercream.

10. To decorate the cake, spoon warm chocolate glaze into a small pastry bag or paper piping cone (see Finishing Touches, page 70). Pipe 3 long-stemmed, open flowers in the middle of the cake. Pipe a scalloped or dotted border of chocolate glaze around the outside rim. Refrigerate the cake briefly to set the chocolate. Serve slightly chilled or at room temperature. Store leftover cake, covered with a cake bell, in the refrigerator for up to 4 days.

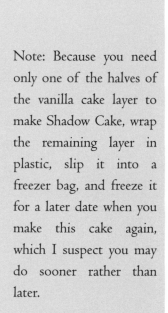

Note: Because you need only one of the halves of the vanilla cake layer to make Shadow Cake, wrap the remaining layer in plastic, slip it into a freezer bag, and freeze it for a later date when you make this cake again, which I suspect you may do sooner rather than later.

FINISHING TOUCHES

To "finish," meaning finish the decoration on a cake, a small pastry bag is frequently recommended. First, it is easier to hold and manipulate than a large pastry bag, making it better suited for fine lines and intricate designs. Second, a small bag requires much less filling, again making it easier to control. When you need a small pastry bag, as for Shadow Cake on page 68, you can create one out of parchment paper. Cut a piece about 6 inches wide by the length of the roll, and roll it into a tight cone, leaving a small opening at the bottom. Tape the cone closed on the side. Spoon melted chocolate or chocolate glaze, as for Shadow Cake, into the cone and fold over the top. Then, holding the bag in one hand, pipe your design.

Vanilla Cake with Ganache Filling and Chocolate Glaze

MAKES ONE 3-LAYER 9-INCH
CAKE, 12 TO 16 SERVINGS

This makes the most fabulous birthday cake. It is beyond rich, and beautiful, just what a birthday cake should be. My pareve "ganache" serves as the filling and the first frosting, then a layer of chocolate glaze seals the outside. To make this cake even richer (*grander* is a better word), use chocolate mousse for the filling. The ganache still plays its part, just a slightly smaller one. You won't believe how delicious the ganache is under that layer of chocolate glaze—it's like having a little bit of chocolate truffle before the first bite of cake.

> 1 Vanilla Cake (page 52), cooled
> About 1 cup Orange-Scented Sugar Syrup (optional, page 94)
> 1 recipe Dr. Paul's "Ganache" (page 100)
> 1 recipe Chocolate Glaze (page 102), not made in advance, but as directed in Step 7

I. With a long-bladed serrated knife, horizontally slice off the crown of the cake to make a level layer. With the knife, slice the cake into 3 equal layers. Place the layers on top of each other and trim the edges of hardened crust all the way around. Reserve the trimmings for making cake crumbs in a bag in the freezer, if desired.

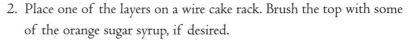

2. Place one of the layers on a wire cake rack. Brush the top with some of the orange sugar syrup, if desired.

3. Measure about 1½ cups of the ganache and spread it evenly over the cake layer.

4. Brush the top of another cake layer with sugar syrup, if using, then invert it onto the ganache. Brush the cake with sugar syrup.

5. Top the cake with another 1½ cups ganache, brush the remaining cake layer with sugar syrup, and invert it onto the ganache. Brush the surface of the top layer with sugar syrup.

6. With a metal spatula, spread the remaining ganache evenly over the sides and top of the cake. Place the cake in the refrigerator and let the ganache set.

7. Because you need to use the chocolate glaze while it is still warm and pourable, make it while the cake chills. It should be warm to the touch, not hot.

8. To glaze the cake: Place a large baking sheet on the work surface. Balancing the wire rack with the cake on the palm of one hand and holding the pan of warm chocolate glaze in the other, pour the glaze over the cake, tilting it as you do so that the glaze runs over the top and cascades down the sides of the cake. Hold the cake over the baking sheet so that the drippings fall onto the sheet. Keep tilting the cake and pouring additional glaze on until the entire surface, including the sides, is covered. The cake will have a thick, glossy, shiny coating. With a spatula, scrape up the cooled glaze on the baking sheet and return it to the pan. Carefully transfer the cake to a cake stand or cake plate. Serve. Store leftover cake, covered with a cake bell or lightly with plastic wrap, in the refrigerator for 4 days.

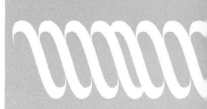

On Melting Chocolate

Chocolate can be temperamental. If subjected to too high a heat when melted, it can "seize," turning granular and bumpy. For all intents and purposes, it is then unusable. To avoid all possibility of that happening, I like to melt chocolate one step removed from direct heat, in the top of a double boiler set over hot, not steaming, water. Stir the chocolate occasionally, until melted, and be sure to keep the water in the bottom of the boiler at a low simmer. When water in the bottom of the boiler boils over high heat, steam forms, and some of the condensation may drop into the chocolate, which can cause the chocolate to seize.

You can also melt chocolate in a microwave oven. Follow the directions on the package of chocolate.

Lastly, you can use the oven. Simply place the chocolate in a heatproof bowl in an oven preheated to 250 degrees.

The least preferred way to melt chocolate is over direct heat. However, if you choose to melt it that way, be sure to use a heavy-bottomed pan over *low* heat.

Chocolate, no matter how you melt it, does so more quickly if broken into small pieces.

Specialty Cakes

Doris's Blackout Cake

MAKES ONE 3-LAYER 10-INCH
CAKE, 12 TO 16 (GENEROUS)
SERVINGS

My father-in-law, the late Itzak Schechter, was a marvelous man, one of my most favorite people in the world. Every Sunday, for many years, he would come to visit us in our house in King's Point. He would bring with him boxes of diamond-shaped sugar cookies from the Hungarian bakery in his neighborhood in Brooklyn. Mixed in with all those boxes was a green-and-white box from Ebinger's, the renowned Brooklyn bakery, containing their famous crumb-covered blackout cake. There was not another chocolate cake like it for miles. All you had to do was ask anyone who had ever tasted an Ebinger's Blackout! Times changed. Ebinger's went out of business. I opened up my own bakery. This is my version of that sinfully rich chocolate cake.

> 1 Chocolate Cake (page 54), cooled
> About ¾ cup Orange-Scented Sugar Syrup (optional, page 94)
> 1 recipe Chocolate Pudding (page 96)

1. With a long-bladed serrated knife, horizontally slice off the crown of the cake to make a level layer. Be sure to reserve the trimmings (they become the crumbs).

2. With the knife, slice the cake into 3 thin, even layers. Reassemble the layers on top of each other and trim the edges of any hardened crust all the way around. Add all the trimmings to the reserved crown and hold at room temperature.

3. Place one of the layers on a cake stand or cake plate. Brush the top lightly with some of the orange sugar syrup, if desired. Measure about ¾ cup of the chocolate pudding and spread it evenly over the layer.

4. Brush one of the remaining cake layers with sugar syrup, if using, then invert it onto the cake on top of the pudding. Brush with sugar syrup.

5. Take another ¾ cup pudding and spread it evenly over the cake. Brush the remaining cake layer with sugar syrup and invert it onto the pudding, as described in Step 4. Brush with sugar syrup.

6. With a metal spatula, spread the remaining chocolate pudding evenly over the sides and top of the cake, using it as frosting.

7. Over a piece of parchment paper or small baking sheet, rub the reserved cake trimmings gently between the palms of your hands, crushing them to make fine cake crumbs. (You should have about 1½ cups crumbs.)

8. Dust the top and sides of the cake with the crumbs, covering it completely. Store leftover cake, covered with a cake bell or lightly with plastic wrap, in the refrigerator for 5 days, or perhaps as long as 1 week.

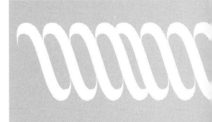

Dr. Paul's Rich Chocolate Cake

MAKES ONE 2-LAYER 9-INCH
CAKE, 12 TO 14 SERVINGS

One day, quite a few years ago now, I received a request from my friend Paula for a very rich, dense chocolate cake that she wanted for her husband's thirtieth birthday. One thing came to mind immediately: The recipe had to include ganache. It took quite a few tries to transform ganache from a dairy recipe to pareve, but with each try we got closer and closer. (See page 100 for the final result.) The finished cake, tied with a chocolate ribbon, turned out to be such a hit—"Dr. Paul" loved it so much—that I named it after him.

If you prefer not to make the chocolate ribbon, here's an easy, also-festive alternative: Place about two dozen whole, chocolate-dipped strawberries in concentric circles over the top of the cake. Or, simpler still, arrange whole undipped strawberries on the cake and drizzle them with melted chocolate.

1 recipe Chocolate Cake batter (page 54)
About ½ cup Orange-Scented Sugar Syrup (optional, page 94)
1 recipe Dr. Paul's "Ganache" (page 100)
1 recipe Chocolate Glaze (page 102), not made ahead of time, but as directed in Step 7

1. Preheat the oven to 350 degrees F. Grease the bottom and sides of two 9-inch cake pans. Cut a round of parchment paper to fit the bottom of each of the pans and line each of the pans. Do not grease the paper.

2. Divide the chocolate batter evenly between the prepared cake pans. Bake the layers for about 30 minutes, or until a cake tester inserted in the center of each of the layers comes out clean. Let the cakes cool in the pans for 5 minutes, invert them out of the pans onto a cake rack, then turn the layers right side up. Let the cakes cool completely.

3. With a long-bladed serrated knife, horizontally slice off the crown on each cake to make a level layer. Place the layers on top of one another and trim the edges of any hardened crust all the way around. Collect all the trimmings, place them in a freezer bag, and freeze. (Use the trimmings for the crumb covering on Doris's Blackout Cake on page 75.)

4. Place one of the layers on a wire cake rack. Brush the top of the layer lightly with some of the orange sugar syrup, if desired. Place about 2 cups of the ganache on the cake and spread it in a thick, even layer over the surface to the edges.

5. Brush the top of the remaining cake layer with sugar syrup, then invert it onto the ganache filling. Brush the top of that layer with sugar syrup.

6. Measure out about 1½ cups of the remaining ganache and use it to frost the sides and top of the cake. Frost the cake in a smooth, even layer. Place the cake in the refrigerator—be sure not to use the freezer—for about 5 minutes for the ganache to set.

7. While the cake is chilling, make the chocolate glaze. You need to use it warm so that it is pourable. It must not be hot.

8. To glaze the cake: Place a large baking sheet on the work surface. Balancing the wire rack with the cake on it on the palm of one

hand and holding the pan of warm chocolate glaze in the other, pour the glaze over the cake, tilting it as you do so that the glaze runs over the top and down the sides of the cake. Hold the cake over the baking sheet so that the drippings fall onto the sheet. Keep tilting the cake and pouring on additional glaze until the entire surface, including the sides, is fully covered. The cake will have a thick, glossy, shiny coating. You will have used about 1½ cups glaze. With a spatula, scrape up the cooled glaze on the baking sheet and return it to the pan. Keep the remaining glaze warm.

9. Place the cake in the refrigerator to set the glaze and to chill slightly. Place a baking sheet in the freezer.

10. To finish the cake with a chocolate ribbon: Measure 2 strips of parchment paper, each 4 inches high by 16 inches long, and cut each out with kitchen shears.

11. Cover the work surface with a large piece of parchment paper. Place the 2 strips on the paper. With a metal spatula, paint each strip evenly with a thin layer of warm chocolate glaze, covering the surface entirely. Lift each chocolate-painted strip of paper off the work surface and place it, paper side down, on the chilled baking sheet in the freezer. Let set in the freezer for about 1 minute—no longer. You are chilling the chocolate, not letting it freeze.

12. Remove the cake from the refrigerator and the chocolate strips from the freezer. Carefully transfer the cake to a cake stand or cake plate. Place one of the strips, chocolate side in, up against the side of the cake, gently pressing it on and around. Remove the paper backing. Where the first strip ends, start the remaining strip, pressing it onto the sides of the cake. Remove that paper backing. The cake has a high-standing chocolate ribbon that now wraps around the cake. Serve. Store leftover cake, covered with a cake bell, in the refrigerator for 4 days.

Royal Aspirations

If you want to give this cake an imperial touch, fashion the ribbon to have peaks like a crown. Cut out the 2 strips of parchment paper as directed in Step 10. Fold each strip in half, and then in half again. Cut out a semicircle in the top of each piece. When you open up the strip, you will have a scalloped edge at the top. Coat the strips with chocolate, chill, and attach to the cake as directed in Steps 11 and 12.

Doris's Sacher Torte

MAKES ONE 2-LAYER 10-INCH
CAKE, 12 TO 16 SERVINGS

Having been born in Vienna and having heard about the famous torte from the Sacher Hotel there ever since I could remember, I felt compelled to create my own Sacher Torte when I opened my bakery. The garnish of meringue mushrooms has become something of a trademark of mine. With or without the mushrooms, this cake is special.

> 1 Chocolate Cake (page 54), cooled
> About 1 cup Orange-Scented Sugar Syrup, or more
>   as desired (optional, page 94)
> ¾ cup raspberry preserves, with seeds or seedless,
>   or apricot preserves
> About 1 cup Dr. Paul's "Ganache" (page 100)
> 1 recipe Chocolate Glaze (page 102)
> 3 or 4 Meringue Mushrooms (optional, page 103)

I. With a long-bladed serrated knife, horizontally slice off the crown of the cake to make a level layer. (Trimmed, the cake will be about 1¼ inches high.) Reserve the trimmings. With the knife, slice the cake into 2 equal layers. With the layers on top of each other, trim the edges of any hardened crust all the way around. Collect all the trimmings, place them in a freezer bag, and freeze. (Use the trimmings for the crumb covering on Doris's Blackout Cake on page 75.)

2. Place one of the layers on a wire cake rack. Brush the top generously with some of the orange sugar syrup, if desired. Spread the raspberry jam in an even layer on top of the cake layer as the filling.

3. Brush the top of the remaining cake layer with some of the sugar syrup, then invert the layer onto the jam. Brush the top with sugar syrup.

4. With a metal spatula, frost the sides and top of the cake with the ganache, spreading it in a smooth, even layer. Place the cake in the refrigerator and let it chill thoroughly before glazing it, about 1 hour.

5. To glaze the cake: Have the chocolate glaze warm enough to pour. Place a large baking sheet on the work surface. Balancing the wire rack with the cake on it on the palm of one hand and holding the pan of warm chocolate glaze in the other, pour the glaze over the cake, tilting it as you do so that the glaze runs over the top and down the sides of the cake. Be sure to hold the cake over the baking sheet so that the drippings fall onto the sheet. Keep tilting the cake and pouring additional glaze on until the entire surface, including the sides, is fully covered. The cake will have a thick, glossy, shiny coating. With a spatula, scrape up the cooled glaze on the baking sheet and place it in a bowl. Cover and reserve in the refrigerator for another use.

6. Place the cake briefly in the refrigerator to allow the glaze to set.

7. Carefully transfer the cake to a cake stand or cake plate. Garnish the cake with the meringue mushrooms, if desired, placing them in a cluster in the center or slightly off to the side. Serve. Store leftover cake, covered with a cake bell or lightly with plastic wrap, in the refrigerator for up to 4 days.

Dumont
Torte

MAKES ONE 10-INCH TART, 8 TO
10 SERVINGS

I first tasted this torte—with its pastry crust, chocolate and almond filling, and drizzle of chocolate on top—at a hotel in Alassio, Italy, on the Ligurian coast. I fell in love with it and immediately asked to speak to the pastry chef. He very generously gave me the recipe, which I promptly brought home and adapted to pareve. To taste it at its absolute best, serve it warm, when the chocolate in the filling is still melted. How it came to be called "Dumont" I don't know. I can only guess that it has something to do with a mountain—or the heights. In my estimation, this torte does soar!

DOUGH
8 tablespoons (1 stick) unsalted margarine
¾ cup sugar
2 large egg yolks
2 cups all-purpose flour

FILLING
8 tablespoons (1 stick) unsalted margarine
¾ cup sugar
2 extra-large eggs, separated
1 tablespoon flour

1½ cups very finely ground unblanched almonds
1¼ teaspoons freshly grated orange zest
2 ounces semisweet chocolate, finely chopped

FINISH
1 ounce bittersweet chocolate, melted and warm
    enough to drizzle

1. Preheat the oven to 350 degrees F. Grease the bottom and sides of a 10-inch fluted tart pan with a removable bottom. Be sure that the sides are greased lightly but thoroughly.

2. Make the dough: In the bowl of a standing electric mixer fitted with the paddle attachment, cream the margarine and sugar on medium speed until fluffy and light. With the machine running, beat in the egg yolks, 1 at a time, beating well after each addition.

3. Turn off the machine, add the flour all at one time, and beat on low speed until the mixture comes together into a dough. With your hand, knead the dough briefly in the bowl until firm. Remove the dough from the bowl and shape it into a disk.

4. On a lightly floured surface, roll the dough into a round about 11 inches in diameter, ¼ inch thick. Transfer the dough to the prepared tart pan and press it gently over the bottom and up the sides of the pan. With a pastry scraper or with the rolling pin, trim the overhang even with the edge of the pan. Reserve the trimmings for making cut-out cookies, if desired. Place the pan in the refrigerator while you make the filling.

5. Make the filling: In the bowl of the standing mixer, cream the margarine and sugar on medium speed until light and fluffy. Add the egg yolks, 1 at a time, beating well after each addition. Beat in the flour and the ground almonds and blend until incorporated. Blend in the orange zest. Transfer the mixture to a large bowl.

6. Wash out the mixer bowl and pat it dry. Fit the mixer with the whisk attachment. Place the 2 egg whites in the bowl and beat on high speed until stiff and glossy. Fold the egg whites into the almond batter.

7. Add the chopped chocolate to the batter and fold it in thoroughly. Pour the filling into the chilled shell and spread it to the edges of the pan. Place the tart pan on a baking sheet.

8. Bake the torte for 45 to 50 minutes until golden and slightly crusty on top. Remove the torte to a rack and let it cool slightly until still just warm to the touch.

9. To finish: Remove the sides of the tart pan. Drizzle the melted chocolate, from the tines of a fork, over the top of the torte. Place the torte on a serving plate and serve in small wedges. Store leftover torte, covered with plastic wrap, in the refrigerator for 2 days.

Viennese
Linzertorte

MAKES ONE 10-INCH TART, 8 TO
10 SERVINGS

Even though I was born in Vienna and my parents were both Austrian, I had never baked a Linzertorte until I lived in Great Neck. The first one I ever made was so beautiful, with its lattice top and diamonds of raspberry jam, I have been making it ever since. It is still one of my most favorite recipes. It is also an old-fashioned one, as you will see from the use of hard-boiled egg yolks in the pastry.

You will not believe how delicious your house will smell when you bake this. The combination of cinnamon, nutmeg, and raspberry is sublime. This is a very special dessert, perfect for occasions of any kind. And, if you love Linzertorte as much as I do, try my Linzer Cookies (page 177). The dough for the cookies is slightly different from the one for this torte.

$1\frac{1}{2}$ cups all-purpose flour

$\frac{1}{4}$ teaspoon ground cinnamon

$\frac{1}{8}$ teaspoon ground nutmeg

1 cup very finely ground (but not to powder) unblanched almonds

$\frac{1}{2}$ pound (2 sticks) unsalted margarine

$\frac{1}{2}$ cup sugar

2 extra-large eggs

(ingredients continued)

1 teaspoon pure vanilla extract
1 teaspoon freshly grated lemon zest
2 hard-cooked large egg yolks, mashed
1 jar (12 ounces) raspberry preserves
Egg wash of 1 egg white

1. Into a large bowl, sift the flour, cinnamon, and nutmeg. Add the ground almonds and stir to combine.

2. In the bowl of a standing electric mixer fitted with the paddle attachment, cream the margarine and the sugar on medium speed until fluffy and light. Scrape down the sides of the bowl with a rubber spatula.

3. Reduce the speed to low and add the eggs, 1 at a time, beating well after each addition. Beat in the vanilla and the lemon zest.

4. Beat in the mashed egg yolks until incorporated. Scrape down the sides of the bowl with the spatula.

5. Turn off the machine and add all the dry ingredients at one time. Turn the machine on to low and beat until a dough forms around the paddle. Scrape the dough off the paddle and shape it into a disk. Wrap the disk in plastic wrap and chill it for at least 1 hour, or until firm.

6. Preheat the oven to 350 degrees F. Lightly dust with flour a 10-inch fluted tart pan with a removable bottom.

7. Remove the chilled dough from the refrigerator and divide it into 2 pieces: The largest piece should be about three-quarters of the dough. On a lightly floured surface, roll the dough into a round about 11 inches in diameter, ¼ inch thick. Gently roll the dough over the rolling pin and center it over the tart pan. Press the dough evenly over the bottom and up the sides. With a pastry cutter or with the rolling pin, trim the overhang even with the edge of the tart pan. With a spatula, spread the raspberry jam evenly over the bottom of the tart pan, covering the dough.

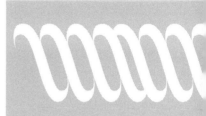

8. Make the lattice top: Roll the remaining smaller piece of dough on a lightly floured surface into a 12-inch square. Using a pizza cutter or fluted pastry cutter and a ruler, cut the square into 8 strips, each about ¾ inch wide.

9. Lightly beat the egg white. With a pastry brush, brush the edge of the dough all the way around the tart pan.

10. Lay 4 of the strips, 1 at a time, spacing them evenly, over the top of the tart; press the strips on the bottom crust to adhere to the egg wash on the edge of the pan. Turn the tart a quarter turn and arrange the remaining 4 strips on the tart, at an angle to the first strips, making a lattice top; firmly press each strip onto the bottom crust. Trim the overhangs of the strips with a dough scraper, reserving the trimmings for another use. With the pastry brush, lightly brush the strips with egg wash.

11. Bake the tart on the middle rack of the oven for about 45 minutes, or until the pastry is lightly golden. Remove the tart to a rack to cool. Before serving, remove the sides of the pan and place the tart on a serving plate. Serve. Store leftover tart, covered with plastic wrap, in the refrigerator for up to 3 days.

VARIATION

A simple adjustment converts this recipe into a stunning dessert for Passover

Substitute 1½ cups matzo cake meal for the flour. Proceed with the recipe as directed.

Fillings, Frostings, and Decorations

Loaf cakes, as we have seen on pages 20 to 46, are best served plain or dusted with confectioners' sugar. Not so layer cakes. They require assembly, and it is how they are assembled, the choices of frosting, filling, and decoration, that make a cake memorable. The frosting, of course, makes the first impression. The filling, hidden from sight, serves as a discovery, and is intended to complement the flavors and textures of the other components. The parts truly make the whole.

A word about my frostings, or "buttercreams": Time and energy went into adapting the famous French *crème au beurre* to pareve. I still call it buttercream, but have put the name in quotation marks because it is made with margarine, not butter. Does my basic vanilla "buttercream" have the velvety smoothness of the original? Yes. Does it take well to flavoring? It does, as you will see when you taste my chocolate, mocha, lemon, and orange variations. Does it make a cake look beautiful? Any one of the five recipes included here assuredly does.

Which brings me to the filling: I think of it as the secret ingredient, and I want to point out two wonderful ones: Dr. Paul's "Ganache" and Chocolate Mousse. While both have been adapted to pareve, each has depth and richness. One bite of Shadow Cake, page 68, with its filling of chocolate mousse (between two different types of cake and its frosting of vanilla "buttercream"), says it all.

Don't worry if you don't succeed at finishing a cake perfectly on the first couple of tries. Frosting a cake, or decorating one, takes practice. You can always add fresh fruit, such as long-stemmed strawberries or fresh raspberries, or even shaved chocolate to the top.

Vanilla "Buttercream"

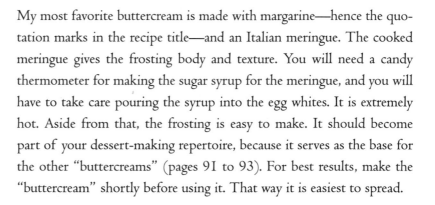

MAKES 3 CUPS, ENOUGH FOR A
TWO- OR THREE-LAYER 9- OR
10-INCH CAKE

My most favorite buttercream is made with margarine—hence the quotation marks in the recipe title—and an Italian meringue. The cooked meringue gives the frosting body and texture. You will need a candy thermometer for making the sugar syrup for the meringue, and you will have to take care pouring the syrup into the egg whites. It is extremely hot. Aside from that, the frosting is easy to make. It should become part of your dessert-making repertoire, because it serves as the base for the other "buttercreams" (pages 91 to 93). For best results, make the "buttercream" shortly before using it. That way it is easiest to spread.

> **4 extra-large egg whites, at room temperature**
> **2 tablespoons water**
> **½ cup sugar**
> **½ pound (2 sticks) unsalted margarine, cut into chunks**
> **2 tablespoons pure vanilla extract**

1. Place the egg whites in the bowl of a standing electric mixer fitted with the whisk attachment.
2. In a small saucepan, combine the water and the sugar and bring to a boil over medium heat. Cook, brushing the sides of the pan with a brush dipped in cold water to remove any sugar crystals on the sides, until the sugar is dissolved. Place a candy thermometer in the pan and cook the mixture, undisturbed.

3. When the syrup reaches 240 degrees F on the thermometer, turn the mixer to high speed and start beating the whites.

4. Continue to cook the syrup until it reaches 250 degrees F on the thermometer. At this point, with the machine running, very carefully start pouring the hot syrup into the egg whites. (The syrup is extremely hot and will burn if it splatters.) Pour it in a steady, slow stream. A meringue will form that is fluffy and white. Once all the syrup has been added, continue to beat the meringue until the bottom of the bowl is no longer hot to the touch, about 10 minutes on high speed.

5. Reduce the speed to low and, with the machine running, add all of the margarine at one time. Increase the speed to high to incorporate the margarine. At first, the mixture will look "broken" and almost curdled. Scrape down the sides of the bowl and continue to beat for 1 minute. The frosting will start to combine. Beat for 1 minute and again scrape down the sides of the bowl. Beat for about 1 minute more until smooth.

6. Scrape down the sides of the bowl a final time and beat for 30 seconds. By hand, beat in the vanilla until incorporated. The buttercream is ready to use.

V A R I A T I O N S

Chocolate "Buttercream"

When I first tasted this, I had difficulty knowing whether it was buttercream or mousse, that's how good it is!

Leave the vanilla buttercream in the mixer bowl in which it was made. In the top of a double boiler set over hot water, melt 6 ounces chopped semisweet chocolate, stirring, until smooth and glossy. Cool completely. When the chocolate is at room temperature, turn the electric mixer to medium speed. With the machine running, scrape the cooled semisweet chocolate into the vanilla buttercream and beat on medium speed until just incorporated. Scrape down the sides of the bowl with a rubber spatula and whisk again to make sure that there are no streaks of chocolate. The buttercream is ready to use. Makes about 4 cups.

Mocha "Buttercream"

I love the pronounced flavor of coffee in this buttercream. If you want a more subtle coffee taste, add half the amount of instant coffee called for, taste, and adjust as desired.

Leave the vanilla buttercream in the mixer bowl in which it was made. Melt the 6 ounces chopped semisweet chocolate as for Chocolate "Buttercream." Stir 3 level tablespoons instant coffee into the warm melted chocolate. Mix into the vanilla buttercream as directed in the recipe for chocolate buttercream. Makes about 4 cups.

Lemon "Buttercream"

This makes the perfect frosting for a simple Génoise layer cake (page 56). It is also very good on Carrot Cake (page 32), as my friend Carla pointed out, after ordering the combination to serve at a pareve meal.

Leave the vanilla buttercream in the mixer bowl in which it was made. Add the finely grated zest and strained juice of 1½ large lemons and beat on medium speed until just incorporated. The buttercream is ready to use. Makes about 3 cups.

Orange "Buttercream"

This buttercream makes a lovely frosting for Orange Cake (page 61), Vanilla Cake (page 52), and Chocolate Cake (page 54).

Leave the vanilla buttercream in the mixer bowl in which it was made. Add ½ cup thawed undiluted orange juice concentrate and the grated zest of 1 large orange and mix on medium speed until just incorporated. The buttercream is ready to use. Makes a little more than 3 cups.

Orange-Scented
Sugar Syrup

Before I went into business and was baking at home, I never used sugar syrup, or simple syrup as it is sometimes called. I didn't see the need for it. Over the years and after listening to many fine bakers, I have come to realize just how useful it is. Brushed on cake layers, it helps prevent them from drying out and can keep them tasting fresh for several days. Depending upon what other ingredient has been added to it, a good syrup can also impart flavor to the cake layers.

> 2 cups water
> 1 cup sugar
> Peel of ½ medium orange

TO STORE

Remove the orange peel from the cooled syrup, transfer the syrup to a jar with a tight-fitting lid, and store in the refrigerator for up to 3 weeks.

In a medium heavy-bottomed saucepan, bring the water, sugar, and orange peel to a boil, stirring and washing down any sugar crystals on the sides of the pan with a pastry brush. Cook, stirring, until the sugar is dissolved. Then cook, without stirring, for about 5 minutes. Remove the pan from the heat and let the syrup cool. The syrup is ready to use.

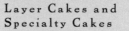

VARIATION

Lemon Sugar Syrup

Make the sugar syrup as directed, omitting the orange peel. Let cool, then stir in ½ cup strained fresh lemon juice (about 2 large lemons). Use or store as directed. Makes about 3 cups.

Chocolate Pudding

I originally developed this chocolate pudding as a component for my Blackout Cake (page 75), then realized it can stand alone. I like to serve it in parfait or pudding glasses, the old-fashioned, cut-glass variety. You can also use wineglasses.

> 2 cups cold water plus ½ cup
> 2 tablespoons unsalted margarine, cut into pieces
> 6 ounces bittersweet or semisweet chocolate, coarsely chopped
> 1 cup sugar
> ¾ cup unsweetened cocoa powder, sifted
> ⅓ cup cornstarch, sifted

1. In a medium saucepan, combine 2 cups cold water and the margarine over medium heat, stirring, until the margarine melts and the water comes to a boil. Add the chopped chocolate and the sugar, and cook, stirring constantly, until the chocolate has melted and the mixture is smooth.
2. Add the cocoa to the chocolate mixture and stir to combine.
3. In a bowl whisk together ½ cup water and the cornstarch until no lumps show.

4. Increase the heat under the chocolate mixture to medium-high and bring the mixture to a boil, whisking constantly. Add the cornstarch mixture and cook, whisking constantly and vigorously, until the pudding thickens and becomes shiny and smooth, 2 to 4 minutes. (Be sure to whisk the bottom and sides of the pan or the pudding will cook onto them.) Remove the pan from the heat.

5. Scrape the pudding into a large heatproof bowl and smooth the top. Press a piece of plastic wrap directly on the surface of the pudding to prevent a skin from forming and let the pudding cool. The pudding is ready to use as a filling or frosting. Or chill and serve at another time as a pudding.

Chocolate Mousse

&

Makes about 5 cups, 8
generous ½-cup servings

When I first made chocolate mousse, I served it for dessert in a lovely crystal bowl. Using it as a pareve cake filling and frosting came later and required some rethinking on my part: A classic dessert mousse is made with either whipped cream or stiffly beaten egg whites. To approximate the lusciousness of heavy cream without using it, I turned to whole eggs and two different types of chocolate—always a safe bet in my book. The adaptations worked beautifully.

If you serve this as dessert, garnish it with fresh raspberries or strawberries—not just for the aesthetic appeal, but for how the flavors and textures enhance each another.

> 6 ounces bittersweet or semisweet chocolate,
>   coarsely chopped
> 2 ounces unsweetened chocolate, coarsely chopped
> 8 tablespoons (1 stick) unsalted margarine
> 6 extra-large eggs, separated
> ¼ cup plus ½ cup sugar

1. In the top of a large double boiler set over hot water, melt both chocolates, stirring, until smooth. Remove the top from the double boiler and let stand on the counter until completely cool.

2. In the bowl of a standing electric mixer fitted with the paddle attachment, cream the margarine on medium speed until very soft, scraping down the sides of the bowl as needed. Add the melted chocolate and beat to combine. Scrape the mixture into a large bowl.

3. Wash the bowl of the mixer and fit the mixer with the whisk attachment.

4. In a medium saucepan, combine the 6 egg yolks with ¼ cup sugar and heat over medium heat, whisking constantly, until the mixture is just warm when tested on your wrist. Do not overheat or the yolks will scramble. Pour the warmed yolk mixture into the mixer bowl and beat on medium-high speed until lemon colored, 2 to 3 minutes. Add the beaten yolks to the melted chocolate mixture and stir until completely incorporated.

5. Wash the mixer bowl and whisk attachment well. Refit the machine with the whisk attachment. Place the egg whites in the bowl and beat them on high speed until very frothy. With the machine running, gradually add ½ cup sugar, beating on high speed until the meringue is stiff, glossy, and holds peaks when you sweep your finger or the whisk attachment through it.

6. Stir about one-quarter of the meringue into the chocolate mixture to lighten it, then gently but thoroughly fold in the remaining meringue until no streaks of chocolate or meringue show. The mousse is ready to use. Or cover the mousse with plastic wrap and store in the refrigerator for up to 1 week.

Dr. Paul's "Ganache"

MAKES ABOUT 4½ CUPS

My goal as owner of a kosher bakery has been to create nondairy cakes by using as many natural ingredients as I could to replicate the taste and texture of the original dairy ingredients. Classic ganache is a rich chocolate filling that consists of nothing more than melted chocolate and heavy cream. To duplicate its luxurious taste without using heavy cream, I've relied on lots of chocolate and eggs. The final result is a winner. At Passover, I like to use this "ganache" as a filling for my Sponge Cake (page 204).

I originally developed this filling for a special birthday cake called Dr. Paul's Rich Chocolate Cake. You can find that chocolate extravaganza on page 77.

> 1 cup water
> ¾ pound (12 ounces) unsweetened chocolate, coarsely chopped
> ¾ cup sugar
> 1 cup freshly brewed strong coffee
> 6 extra-large eggs, whisked together well

1. In the top of a large double boiler set over hot water, bring the water to a boil.

2. In a bowl combine the chocolate and the sugar.

3. Add the chocolate and sugar mixture plus the coffee to the water in the top of the double boiler and cook, stirring, until the sugar has dissolved and the chocolate has melted.

4. Pour the beaten eggs through a fine-meshed sieve into the hot chocolate mixture and cook, stirring constantly, until thickened and puddinglike in consistency, 10 to 15 minutes. Remove the top of the double boiler and spoon the mixture into a large bowl to cool. When completely cool, cover with plastic wrap and refrigerate. Properly stored, the ganache keeps for up to 1 week.

Chocolate Glaze

MAKES ABOUT 2¼ CUPS

Many chocolate glazes are made by melting chocolate with butter and, sometimes but not always, a flavoring. My glaze is almost pure chocolate, a pound of it. The corn syrup lends just enough texture so that the glaze pours like a dream when warm, covering whatever you use it on with an even, luscious, thick layer. I love using this glaze to finish special-occasion cakes, like my Sacher Torte (page 80). It is also great on humble cupcakes.

1 pound semisweet chocolate, coarsely chopped
½ cup boiling water
¼ cup light corn syrup

TO STORE

Cover the bowl well with plastic wrap and store it in the refrigerator. Reheat over low heat, stirring, until warm enough to pour.

1. In the top of a large double boiler set over hot water, melt the chocolate, stirring, until smooth and glossy. Transfer the chocolate to a large heatproof bowl.
2. Gradually whisk the boiling water into the melted chocolate. (At first the chocolate will look lumpy and almost as if it has "seized." With continued whisking, it will become smooth.)
3. When the mixture is smooth, add the corn syrup and whisk it in completely. The glaze will be slightly thicker, shiny, and smooth.
4. Set a fine-meshed sieve over a medium heatproof bowl. Pour the still-warm glaze through the sieve into the bowl, pressing it through with the back of a large metal spoon. The glaze should be used while it is still warm and easily pourable.

Meringue Mushrooms

I can't remember where I first saw meringue mushrooms, but I do remember thinking how pretty they were and that I had to learn how to make them. When I placed a few of them in a cluster on my Sacher Torte (page 80), they quickly became a trademark of mine.

Set out a plate of these little meringues to have with after-dinner coffee. They are especially good after a rich dinner because they are so light.

> 1 recipe Vanilla Meringues batter (page 232)
> About 2 tablespoons unsweetened cocoa powder, for
> dusting
> 2 ounces semisweet chocolate, melted but still
> warm, for assembling the mushrooms

1. Preheat the oven to 250 degrees F. Line 2 large baking sheets with parchment paper.
2. Spoon the meringue batter into a large pastry bag fitted with a large plain tip. To make the "caps" of the mushrooms, pipe round mounds, each about 1 inch wide and ¾ inch high, in rows onto a prepared sheet. Leave at least ½ inch in between. Pipe 48 mounds.
3. To make the mushroom "stems," pipe smaller mounds with peaks, each about ¾ inch high, in rows onto the other prepared sheet, leaving at least ½ inch in between. (The mounds should resemble Hershey's chocolate kisses in size and shape.) Pipe 48 stems.

103

4. Place the cocoa powder in a fine-meshed sieve and dust only the mushroom caps with it. Do not dust the stems.

5. Bake the meringues for I hour. Turn off the oven and let the meringues stand in the turned-off oven for another hour to dry. After the meringues have dried, you can assemble the mushrooms, or store the meringues for later assembly.

6. To assemble the mushrooms: With a skewer, poke a hole in the bottom of each of the mushroom caps that is just large enough to hold the peak of a mushroom stem. With the top of a small knife, paint the bottom, except the hole, with a dab of melted chocolate. Put the tip of a mushroom stem into the hole, pressing the parts together gently to stick. Place the mushrooms on a wire rack to dry. Store in an airtight container.

Pies
and Tarts

My Most Favorite Sugar Crust
Rich Pie Dough

PIES
Grandma's Apple "Cake"
Deep-Dish Apple Crumb Pie
Old-Fashioned Apple Pie
Lattice-Top Apple Pie
Lattice-Top Strawberry-Rhubarb Pie
Pumpkin Pie
Pecan Pie

TARTS
Apple Tart
Fresh Fruit Tart
Blueberry Tart
Mixed Berry Tart
Pear Frangipane Tart
Strawberry Tart with Crumb Topping
Lemon Meringue Tart
Plum Tart

Introduction

In summer, pies and tarts head a very short list of my most favorite desserts, falling only to second in winter, when cakes get the nod. I have loved fruits in crust, in particular, ever since I can remember, tracing the start of that affection back to a cake my grandma made with apples. (My variation of that fond memory is on page 113.) The pages that follow show just how partial I am to apples and crust. There are five different apples and crust combinations in all! Not just any crust, though. I prefer sugar crust. It must be rolled quite thick and baked until crunchy to serve not just as a containers but as a foil for the fruit. As pareve recipes go, sugar crust was not hard to develop. From the start, we used margarine, and it worked fine.

One thing a My Most Favorite Dessert Company fruit tart never contains is pareve pastry cream. Long ago I decided that to be as natural as possible, our fruit tarts would contain only fruit. We have never strayed from that goal. We fill a sugar crust shell with a fresh fruit combination and bake it until it is cooked down and almost jamlike. When cool, we top the tart with lots of fresh fruit. With Blueberry Tart, for example, you bite into berries, then into fruit jam, then into crunchy sugar crust—it's a wonderful taste and texture sensation.

If there is one recipe in this whole chapter that I would urge you to make, it is the Lemon Meringue Tart (page 146). At my bakery in Great Neck, I made a dairy lemon tart that I just loved. Never did I imagine that a pareve lemon meringue tart could equal it, but this one does.

My
Most Favorite
Sugar Crust

My father-in-law, a wonderful man, came to King's Point, in Great Neck, often to visit his five grandchildren, and he always brought with him pounds of the best sugar cookies I ever tasted. They were from a Hungarian bakery in Brooklyn, and they melted in your mouth. We all loved them. I remember my children lined up like little soldiers as Izzy handed the cookies out. I was in line, too. I think I could have eaten a whole pound of them on my own. Those unforgettable cookies were the inspiration for this sugar crust, which we use as our all-purpose pie and tart crust. And when I say all-purpose, I really mean *all*-purpose: our best-selling Grandma's Apple "Cake," lattice-top fresh fruit pies, Pecan Pie, and any number of fruit tarts. Not surprisingly, we make Sugar Cookies (page 176) with it, too.

A word of advice before you make the dough: Remove the margarine from the refrigerator right before you plan to use it. Cold margarine creams more efficiently than softened margarine does, and your goal is a well-crafted crust, which begins with the margarine and sugar mixture.

12 tablespoons (1½ sticks) cold unsalted margarine
⅓ cup sugar
1 extra-large egg
½ teaspoon pure vanilla extract
2 cups all-purpose flour

1. In the bowl of a standing electric mixer fitted with the paddle attachment, cream the margarine with the sugar on medium speed until fluffy.
2. In a small bowl, beat the egg together lightly with the vanilla. With the mixer running, add the egg mixture to the margarine mixture and beat until they are incorporated.
3. Reduce the mixer speed to low and add the flour, a cup at a time, beating until a ball of dough forms around the paddle.
4. With your hands, gather the dough into a ball, and pat it into a large, flat round. Divide the round in half, shape each half into a disk, and wrap each disk in plastic wrap. Chill the disks in the refrigerator for at least 2 hours, preferably 3 to 4 hours, or until firm.

TO FREEZE
The dough, wrapped well in plastic wrap, may be frozen for up to 1 month.

TO DEFROST
Thaw in the plastic wrap at room temperature.

Rich
Pie Dough

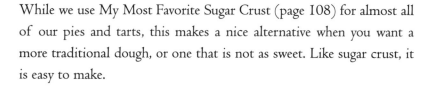

MAKES ENOUGH DOUGH FOR
ONE 9- OR 10-INCH SINGLE-
CRUST PIE

While we use My Most Favorite Sugar Crust (page 108) for almost all of our pies and tarts, this makes a nice alternative when you want a more traditional dough, or one that is not as sweet. Like sugar crust, it is easy to make.

> **14 tablespoons (1¾ sticks) chilled unsalted
>   margarine**
> **2 tablespoons sugar**
> **3 extra-large egg yolks**
> **1 tablespoon water**
> **¾ cup all-purpose flour**

1. In the bowl of a standing electric mixer fitted with the paddle attachment, cream the margarine and the sugar on medium speed until fluffy.
2. In a cup beat together the egg yolks and the water.
3. With the machine running, add the yolk mixture to the bowl and beat until incorporated.
4. Reduce the mixer speed to low and add the flour, a little at a time, beating until a dough forms. Remove the dough from the bowl and knead it several times on the work surface. The dough is ready for

using or can be shaped into a disk, wrapped in plastic wrap, and refrigerated for no more than 1 day.

An Easy Roll

If you are inexperienced at rolling out pie dough or the prospect of doing it makes you nervous, roll out the dough between two sheets of wax paper. Here's why it is a good idea:

- it cuts down on the amount of flour new bakers usually use to flour the work surface (rolling and rerolling the dough, adding more flour each time, makes the dough tough);
- it prevents the dough from sticking to the counter or the rolling pin; and
- it removes the sometimes tricky step of transferring the dough to the baking pan. Instead of rolling the dough loosely around the pin as a means of transferring it, remove the top sheet of wax paper, then center the baking pan on top of the dough. Using the wax paper as an aid, invert the pan with the dough on it right side up. Remove the wax paper and press the dough into the pan as directed.

Tips like these are useful, but if you want to become really good at working with dough there is only one way to do it: practice, over and over again. Eventually you will know when the dough is ready by its appearance and the feel of it in your hands.

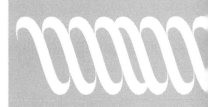

TO FREEZE
Wrap the disk of dough in plastic wrap, place the dough in a freezer bag, and freeze for up to 1 month.

TO DEFROST
Thaw in the plastic wrap at room temperature.

Pies

Grandma's Apple "Cake"

&

MAKES ONE 12 × 7½-INCH PIE,
10 TO 14 SERVINGS

Grandma Leah made her apple cake for holidays and Friday nights. It was flat and thin, with bottom and top crusts, and apples in between. Everyone just loved it. In fact, she used to hide it in her bedroom so that none of the kids would find it. Of course, my sister and I would run right into her bedroom, immediately find where it was, and start to nibble!

This is my interpretation, a variation on the theme of Leah's beloved apple cake. It is similar but different. I use lots and lots of apples and a sugar crust. This is one of our most popular desserts and always has been.

SUGAR CRUST
¾ pound (3 sticks) cold unsalted margarine
⅔ cup sugar
2 extra-large eggs
1 teaspoon pure vanilla extract
4 cups all-purpose flour

APPLE FILLING MIXTURE
¾ cup sugar
9 tablespoons apricot preserves

(ingredients continued)

113

¾ teaspoon ground cinnamon

1½ tablespoons flour

3 tablespoons cornstarch

3 tablespoons water

12 cups peeled medium-thick (½ inch wide)
    McIntosh apple slices (about 12 large apples)

Egg wash of 1 extra-large whole egg, lightly beaten

Sugar, for sprinkling on the crust

1. Make the dough following the directions on page 109. Divide the dough in half, shape each half into a disk, and wrap in plastic wrap. If the dough feels soft and unready for rolling, chill it several hours in the refrigerator or for 1 hour in the freezer.

2. Preheat the oven to 350 degrees F. Line a large baking sheet with parchment paper. Remove the disks of dough from the refrigerator and let them stand at room temperature to soften slightly before rolling out.

3. On a lightly floured surface, roll one of the disks of dough into a rectangle about 14 × 9 inches, ¼ inch thick. Gently roll the dough over the rolling pin and center it over a 12 × 7½-inch rectangular baking pan. Press the dough over the bottom and up the sides. Trim the overhang so that it covers the rim of the pan. Chill the pie shell while you make the filling.

4. Make the apple filling mixture: In a large bowl, stir together the sugar, apricot preserves, cinnamon, and flour until well combined.

5. Put the cornstarch in a small bowl, add the water, and stir until combined and there are no lumps. Stir the cornstarch mixture into the apricot mixture. Add the apple slices and, with your hands, toss until the apples are well coated.

6. Place the apple filling in the lined cake pan, mounding it in the center. (The filling will stand very high in the pan.)

7. With a pastry brush, brush the edge of the dough all the way around with the egg wash.

8. Reflour the work surface lightly and roll out the remaining piece of dough into a 14 × 9-inch rectangle, ¼ inch thick. Roll the dough over the rolling pin and center it over the filling. With your fingers, press the edge of the top crust into the edge of the bottom crust, sealing it at the corners, then all the way around. Trim the edge of the top dough even with the edge of the pan. With the tines of a fork, lightly press the edge of the crust all the way around to seal. Prick the top crust all over with the tines of the fork to make steam vents.

9. Brush the top crust and the edge with egg wash, then sprinkle generously with sugar.

10. Place the pan on the lined baking sheet and bake for 1 hour and 5 to 10 minutes until the top crust is a lovely golden brown. Transfer the cake to a wire rack and let it cool completely. You can also serve it warm. Store leftovers, covered with plastic wrap, in the refrigerator for up to 3 days.

V A R I A T I O N

Grandma's Yom Kippur Apple "Cake"

I like to serve this on the eve of Yom Kippur, the night before the fast, as it is customary to eat bland food to prepare for the day of fasting.

Prepare the sugar crust and line the pan as directed in the recipe. Make the filling: In a large bowl, combine 7 cups peeled medium-thick McIntosh apple slices (about 7 large apples), ¾ cup sugar, 2 teaspoons ground cinnamon, ¾ cup ground blanched almonds, ¾ cup dark raisins, and 1 tablespoon freshly grated lemon zest. Spread the filling over the dough in an even layer. Roll out the remaining dough on a lightly floured surface into a large rectangle about ¼ inch thick. Using a large apple-shaped cookie cutter, about 3½ inches wide and 4 inches high, cut out the dough. (You will need at least 12 cutout dough apples.) Arrange the cutouts lengthwise in rows, overlapping the pieces slightly, to cover the filling completely. Brush the cutouts generously with egg wash, taking care not to disturb the pattern, and sprinkle with plenty of granulated sugar. Place the pan on a baking sheet and bake for 45 to 55 minutes until the top crust is a rich golden brown. Remove to a large wire rack and let cool. Store, covered with plastic wrap, in the refrigerator for up to 3 days.

Vanilla Meringues
page 232

Success Cake
page 212

Viennese Orange Cookies
page 194

Shadow Cake
page 68

Coconut Macaroons
page 226

Viennese Linzertorte
page 85

Doris's Blackout Cake
page 75

Apple Tart
page 133

Linzer Cookies
page 177

Marble Loaf Cake
page 30

Lattice-Top Apple Pie
page 122

My Most Favorite Brownies
page 157

Vanilla Crescent Cookies
page 190

Lemon Meringue Tart
page 146

Plum Tart
page 148

Velvet Chocolate Cake
page 208

Chocolate Chip Sand Tart
page 174

Mixed Berry Tart
page 139

Glazed Orange Bundt Cake
page 38

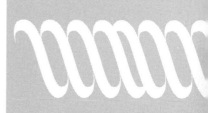

Deep-Dish Apple Crumb Pie

MAKES ONE DEEP-DISH 8-INCH
PIE, 8 TO 10 SERVINGS

Each of my three daughters is a good cook. My daughter Renée is a very talented and experienced baker. She worked at My Most Favorite Dessert Company when we were on Madison Avenue, and memory serves that this recipe is one that she created when a customer asked if we could make an apple crumb pie. Crumb pies, in general, seem to be very popular, and this one especially so. And even though you invert the pie out of the pan, the topping does not fall off.

A slice of this apple crumb pie is just perfect with a cup of tea on a wintry afternoon.

My Most Favorite Sugar Crust (page 108, halving all the ingredients, except for the egg)

APPLE FILLING MIXTURE
¼ cup sugar
3 tablespoons apricot preserves
¼ teaspoon ground cinnamon
½ tablespoon flour
1 tablespoon cornstarch
1 tablespoon water

(ingredients continued)

117

**5 cups peeled medium-thick (½ inch wide) McIntosh
apple slices (about 5 large apples)
1 recipe Crumb Topping (page 144)**

1. Preheat the oven to 350 degrees F. Grease well the bottom and sides of an 8-inch metal cake pan, 3 inches deep.

2. On a lightly floured surface, roll the dough into a round about ¼ inch thick and about 10 inches in diameter. Gently roll the dough over the rolling pin, center it over the cake pan, and unroll it over the pan. Press the dough over the bottom and up the sides. With a fluted pizza cutter or pastry cutter, trim the dough all the way around about ¼ inch from the top edge.

3. Make the apple filling mixture: In a large bowl, combine all the mixture ingredients with the apples and toss until the slices are well coated. Spread the filling evenly in the lined cake pan.

4. Sprinkle the crumb topping evenly over the filling.

5. Place the pan on a baking sheet and bake for about 1 hour and 5 minutes, or until the crumb topping is nicely browned and the crust around the edges is deep golden. Remove the pan from the oven and let cool completely. Place a plate over the pan, invert the pie out of the pan, then set the pie right side up. Serve. Store leftovers, covered with plastic wrap, in the refrigerator for up to 3 days.

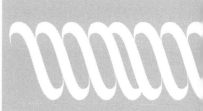

APPLES, APPLES EVERYWHERE

Even though I use McIntosh apples exclusively both in the bakery and for cooking at home, there are a great many other apples on the market, some of which are especially recommended for baking. They include: Jonagold, Macoun, Rome, and Granny Smith (although I personally find the latter too tart). You can always use a combination of several kinds of baking apples, too.

However, be aware that apples that are good for baking are not necessarily good for cooking. Some good cooking apples are Golden Delicious, Idared, and Gala.

McIntoshes still get my vote, because of their flavor and tenderness, but especially because of how they hold their shape when baked.

Old-Fashioned Apple Pie

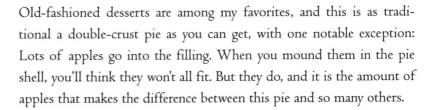

MAKES ONE 2-CRUST 10-INCH
PIE, 10 TO 12 SERVINGS

Old-fashioned desserts are among my favorites, and this is as traditional a double-crust pie as you can get, with one notable exception: Lots of apples go into the filling. When you mound them in the pie shell, you'll think they won't all fit. But they do, and it is the amount of apples that makes the difference between this pie and so many others.

**My Most Favorite Sugar Crust for a 2-crust 10-inch
pie (page 108)**

APPLE FILLING MIXTURE
$\frac{1}{2}$ cup sugar
6 tablespoons apricot preserves
$\frac{1}{2}$ teaspoon ground cinnamon
1 tablespoon flour
2 tablespoons cornstarch
2 tablespoons water

8 cups peeled medium-thick ($\frac{1}{2}$ inch wide) McIntosh
apple slices (about 8 large apples)

Egg wash of 1 whole egg, lightly beaten
Sugar, for sprinkling on the top crust

1. Preheat the oven to 350 degrees F. Line a large baking sheet with parchment paper. Remove the disks of dough from the refrigerator and let them stand at room temperature for 5 to 10 minutes to soften slightly before rolling out.

2. On a lightly floured surface, roll one of the disks of dough into a round about 11 inches in diameter, ¼ inch thick. Gently roll the round over the rolling pin, center it over a 10-inch pie plate, and unroll it over the pan. Press the dough over the bottom and up the sides of the pan. With a pastry scraper or a knife, trim the overhang with the edge of the pan. Chill the pie shell while you make the filling.

3. Make the apple filling mixture: In a large bowl, combine the sugar, apricot preserves, cinnamon, and flour and stir until blended.

4. In a small cup, place the cornstarch, add the water, and stir until there are no lumps. Stir into the apricot mixture. Add the apples and toss gently until well coated. Mound the filling in the pie shell.

5. With a pastry brush, brush the edge of the dough all the way around with egg wash.

6. Reflour the work surface and roll out the remaining disk of dough into a round about 11 inches in diameter, ¼ inch thick. Transfer the round on the rolling pin to the pie and center it over the filling. With your fingers, press the edge of the top crust into the bottom crust all the way around, then trim the overhang. With the tines of a fork, press the edges all the way around to seal. Prick the top crust all over with the tines of the fork to make steam vents.

7. Brush the top crust and edge with the egg wash, then sprinkle it generously with sugar.

8. Place the pie on the lined baking sheet and bake for 50 to 60 minutes until nicely golden on the top. Transfer the pie to a wire rack to cool and serve either warm or at room temperature. Store leftovers, covered with plastic wrap, in the refrigerator for up to 3 days.

Lattice-Top
Apple Pie

When I decided to make apple pie for the bakery—2-crust, lattice-top, or deep-dish—I did a considerable amount of testing on the flavoring for the filling. Too often in apple pies, cinnamon is all you taste. My goal was to make it truly flavor filled—hence the apricot preserves.

**My Most Favorite Sugar Crust for a 2-crust 10-inch
  pie (page 108)**

APPLE FILLING MIXTURE
½ cup sugar
6 tablespoons apricot preserves
½ teaspoon ground cinnamon
1 tablespoon flour
2 tablespoons cornstarch
2 tablespoons water

8 cups peeled medium-thick (½ inch wide) McIntosh
  apple slices (about 8 large apples)

Egg wash of 1 whole egg, lightly beaten
Sugar, for sprinkling on the lattice strips

1. Preheat the oven to 350 degrees F. Remove the dough from the refrigerator and let it stand at room temperature for 5 to 10 minutes to soften before rolling out. Line a baking sheet with parchment paper to catch any juices that may spill over the crust.

2. Working with one disk of dough at a time, roll it out into a round about 11 inches in diameter on a lightly floured surface. Gently roll the dough over the rolling pin, center it over a 10-inch pie plate or pie tin, and unroll the dough over the pan. Press the dough over the bottom and up the sides of the pan. With a dough scraper, trim the overhang, leaving just enough dough to cover the full rim of the pan. Gather up the trimmings and reserve for another use.

3. Make the apple filling mixture: In a large bowl, combine the sugar, apricot preserves, cinnamon, and flour until blended.

4. In a small cup, place the cornstarch, add the water, and stir until there are no lumps. Add to the apricot mixture along with the apples and toss until the slices are well coated. Mound the filling in the pie shell.

5. Make the lattice top: Shape the remaining disk of dough into a cylinder, then roll it into a 10 × 12-inch rectangle on a lightly floured surface. Using a fluted pizza or pie dough cutter and a ruler, cut the rectangle crosswise into 8 one-inch-wide strips.

6. Brush the edge of the crust all the way around with the egg wash. Brush the 8 strips with egg wash, then sprinkle them generously with the sugar. (You should be able to see a thin layer of sugar on the strips.)

7. Lay 4 of the strips, 1 at a time, over the top of the pie, spacing them evenly; press the strips on the bottom crust to adhere to the egg wash on the edge. Turn the pie a quarter turn and arrange the remaining 4 strips on the pie, at an angle to the first strips, making a lattice top; firmly press each strip onto the bottom crust. Trim the overhangs with a dough scraper, reserving them for baking into cookies, if desired.

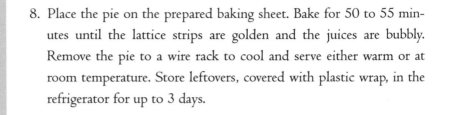

8. Place the pie on the prepared baking sheet. Bake for 50 to 55 minutes until the lattice strips are golden and the juices are bubbly. Remove the pie to a wire rack to cool and serve either warm or at room temperature. Store leftovers, covered with plastic wrap, in the refrigerator for up to 3 days.

VARIATION

Lattice-Top Peach-Plum Pie

Make a filling of 2 cups each of peeled ripe peaches (about 2 large) and sliced red plums (2 to 3 large), ⅔ cup raspberry preserves, and ⅓ cup each of sugar and flour, stirring well to combine. Line the pie shell as directed in Step 2 in the recipe, fill it, and make and glaze the lattice top as directed in Steps 5 through 7. Bake the pie for 40 to 45 minutes until nicely golden on top and the juices are bubbly. Makes 8 to 10 servings.

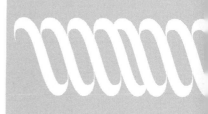

Lattice-Top Strawberry-Rhubarb Pie

MAKES ONE 10-INCH PIE, 8 TO 10 SERVINGS

This is one of our most popular pies, but I must confess that I came to like rhubarb in a roundabout way. When I was young, my grandmother made rhubarb compote. It looked awful and tasted worse! For years, I avoided rhubarb. My daughter Renée convinced me to try *strawberry-rhubarb* pie, and I have loved it ever since. What a difference a few berries can make!

My Most Favorite Sugar Crust for a 2-crust 10-inch pie (page 108)

FILLING
2 cups hulled strawberries, sliced
2 cups chopped frozen but unthawed rhubarb, or fresh rhubarb
⅔ cup sugar
3 tablespoons cornstarch
½ cup raspberry preserves, with or without seeds
Juice of ½ lemon

Egg wash of 1 whole egg, lightly beaten
Sugar, for sprinkling on the lattice strips

1. Preheat the oven to 350 degrees F. Remove the dough from the refrigerator and let it stand at room temperature to soften before rolling out. Line a baking sheet with parchment paper to catch any juices that may spill over the crust.

2. Working with one disk of dough at a time, roll it out into a round about 11 inches in diameter on a lightly floured surface. Gently roll the dough over the rolling pin, center it over a 10-inch pie plate or pie tin, and unroll the dough over the pan. Press the dough over the bottom and up the sides of the pan. With a dough scraper, trim the overhang, leaving just enough dough to cover the full rim of the pan. Gather up the trimmings and reserve for cookies.

3. Make the filling: In a medium bowl, combine the strawberries, rhubarb, sugar, cornstarch, raspberry preserves, and lemon juice, and toss gently to combine and coat the fruit. Spoon the filling into the pie shell.

4. Shape the remaining disk of dough into a cylinder, then roll it into a 10 × 12-inch rectangle on a lightly floured surface. Using a fluted pizza or pie dough cutter and a ruler, cut the rectangle crosswise into 8 one-inch-wide strips.

5. Brush the edge of the crust all the way around with egg wash. Brush the 8 strips with egg wash, then sprinkle them generously with sugar. (You should be able to see a thin layer of sugar on the strips.)

6. Lay 4 of the strips, 1 at a time, over the top of the pie, spacing them evenly; press the strips on the bottom crust to adhere to the egg wash on the edge. Turn the pie a quarter turn and arrange the remaining strips on the pie, at an angle to the first strips, making a lattice top; firmly press each strip onto the bottom crust. Trim the overhangs with a dough scraper, reserving them for baking into cookies.

7. Place the pie on the lined baking sheet. Bake for about 45 minutes, or until the lattice strips are golden and the juices have bubbled up

around the edges. Remove the pie to a wire rack to cool completely before serving. Store leftovers, covered with plastic wrap, in the refrigerator for up to 3 days.

WITH SEEDS OR WITHOUT . . . YOU DECIDE

My husband, Marvin, can't stand biting into the seeds of raspberry preserves and still asks me, after nearly twenty years of being in the baking business, why I use them in so many of my products. I happen to love the seeds. But, if you are like Marvin and dislike them, simply use seedless raspberry preserves, or another kind of preserve.

Pumpkin
Pie

MAKES ONE 10-INCH PIE, 8 TO
10 SERVINGS

One Thanksgiving My Most Favorite Dessert Company got a tremendous number of calls for pumpkin pie. I must admit I had never liked it, but because of the requests I started developing a pareve pumpkin pie. That is how and when my love affair with pumpkin began—with this pie. It tastes so marvelous when made pareve. The filling reminds me of pumpkin mousse.

**Rich Pie Dough (page 110) or My Most Favorite
Sugar Crust (page 108, halving all the
ingredients, except for the egg)**

FILLING
3 extra-large eggs
½ cup firmly packed dark brown sugar
¼ cup granulated sugar
1 can (16 ounces) pumpkin puree (not pumpkin pie
filling)
½ teaspoon ground cinnamon
½ teaspoon ground ginger
½ teaspoon ground nutmeg
½ teaspoon salt
1 cup vanilla soy milk (see headnote, page 26)

1. Preheat the oven to 350 degrees F. Line a baking sheet with parchment paper.

2. On a lightly floured surface, roll the dough into an 11-inch round. Roll the dough lightly over the rolling pin, center it over a 10-inch pie plate, and unroll it over the plate. Gently press the dough over the bottom and up the sides of the pan. Trim the dough all the way around to a ½-inch overhang, then decoratively flute the dough into a high-standing edge. (The fluted edge should stand about ½ inch above the edge of the pan in order to contain the filling.)

3. Make the filling: In a bowl, by hand or using a standing electric mixer fitted with the paddle attachment, combine the eggs, brown sugar, and granulated sugar and beat on medium speed until blended.

4. Add the pumpkin, spices, and salt and beat until the pumpkin is incorporated.

5. Add the soy milk and beat until the filling is combined.

6. Place the pie shell on the lined baking sheet, then pour the filling into the shell. (The filling will come almost to the top of the fluted edge.) Carefully transfer the pie to the oven. Bake for about 45 minutes, or until the filling is set and the crust around the edge is a light golden brown. Remove the pie to a wire rack and let cool completely before serving. Store leftovers, covered with plastic wrap, in the refrigerator for no more than 2 days.

Pecan Pie

MAKES ONE 10-INCH PIE, 8 TO 10 SERVINGS

This pie has pecans not only in the filling, but entirely covering the top. It makes a wonderful pie for Thanksgiving or any other time of year. If you are serving a dairy meal, a dollop of whipped cream or a scoop of vanilla ice cream alongside is very good.

My Most Favorite Sugar Crust (page 108, halving all the ingredients, except for the egg)
1 cup pecan pieces

FILLING
2 tablespoons margarine
3/4 cup light Karo syrup
1/2 cup sugar
Pinch of salt
2 extra-large eggs, beaten lightly
1/2 teaspoon pure vanilla extract
1 1/2 cups whole pecans, for covering the top

1. Preheat the oven to 350 degrees F. Line a baking sheet with parchment paper.
2. On a lightly floured surface, roll the dough into an 11-inch round. Roll the dough lightly over the rolling pin, center it over a 10-inch

pie plate, and unroll it over the plate. Gently press the dough over the bottom and up the sides of the pan. Trim the dough all the way around to a ½-inch overhang, then flute the edge. Spread the broken pecan pieces in an even layer over the bottom of the shell.

3. Make the filling: In a heavy-bottomed saucepan, melt the margarine over low heat. Add the Karo syrup and heat, stirring, until dissolved. Add the sugar and cook over medium heat, stirring, until melted and incorporated. Stir in the salt. Remove the pan from the heat and let the mixture cool, stirring occasionally. When cool, beat in the eggs until incorporated. Stir in the vanilla.

4. Pour the filling into the pie shell; press down on the pecan pieces to cover them and distribute them evenly.

5. Starting at the outside edge, on the filling place the whole pecans, 1 at a time, as close together as possible and facing toward the middle of the pie, making concentric circles, until the entire surface is covered. Place the pie on the lined baking sheet.

6. Bake for 45 minutes, or until the edge of the crust is golden and the pecans on the top are beginning to brown. If need be, to prevent the edge of the crust from overbrowning, cover it with a thin strip of aluminum foil for the last 10 minutes of baking. Remove the pie to a wire rack and let cool completely before serving. Store leftovers, covered with plastic wrap, in the refrigerator for up to 3 days.

Tarts

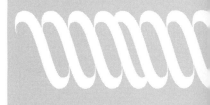

Apple Tart

This tart looks like the apple tarts you see in the *pâtisserie* in Paris. It makes a beautiful presentation and is elegant enough to serve to guests.

MAKES ONE 10-INCH TART, 8 TO 10 SERVINGS

My Most Favorite Sugar Crust (page 108, halving all the ingredients, except for the egg)

APPLE FILLING MIXTURE
½ cup sugar
6 tablespoons apricot preserves
½ teaspoon ground cinnamon
1 tablespoon flour
2 tablespoons cornstarch
2 tablespoons water

5 cups peeled medium-thick (½ inch thick) McIntosh apple slices (about 5 large apples) chopped fine plus 2 medium McIntosh apples, peeled, cored, and very thinly sliced, for decorating the top
Apricot preserves, melted and still warm, for glaze

1. Preheat the oven to 350 degrees F. Remove the dough from the refrigerator and let it stand at room temperature for 5 to 10 minutes to soften before rolling out. Line a baking sheet with parchment paper.

2. On a lightly floured surface, roll the dough into a round about 11 inches in diameter. Lightly roll the dough over the rolling pin, center the rolling pin over a 10-inch fluted tart pan with a removable bottom, and unroll the dough over the pan. Gently press the dough over the bottom and up the sides of the pan. With a pastry scraper or with the rolling pin, trim the overhang of the dough even with the edge of the pan. Refrigerate the shell while you make the filling.

3. Make the apple filling mixture: In a medium bowl, stir together the sugar, apricot preserves, cinnamon, and flour.

4. In a cup place the cornstarch, add the water, and stir until there are no lumps. Stir into the apricot mixture, add the chopped apples, and toss gently until the pieces are coated. Spread the filling evenly over the dough. (It will come right up to the top rim.) Place the pan on the lined baking sheet.

5. For the decorative top: Starting at the outside edge of the tart shell, place a ring of the thin apple slices, overlapping them slightly, on the filling all the way around the tart. Select smaller slices from the remaining apples, and create a flowerlike design in the center, leaning the slices up against each other to make them look like petals.

6. Bake the tart for about 1 hour and 15 minutes, or until the crust is golden and the apples on the top are lightly colored and just starting to caramelize around the edges. After an hour of baking, cover the edge of the dough with a strip of aluminum foil to prevent it from burning. Remove the tart from the oven, brush the apples on top with the warm apricot preserves, and let the tart cool completely on a wire rack. Before serving, remove the sides of the pan and place the tart on a serving plate. Store leftovers, covered with plastic wrap, in the refrigerator for up to 3 days.

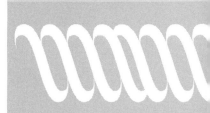

Fresh
Fruit Tart

When we started pareve baking at My Most Favorite Dessert Company, I decided that I would not try to adapt French pastry cream to nondairy, but use a fresh fruit filling instead. It proved to be a good decision: A cooked fruit filling is much easier to prepare and better for you.

Fruit tarts are one of the best desserts I know because they can be adapted in so many ways to the seasons and available fruits. We have made this with sliced mangoes and kiwis, apricots and peaches, nectarines and plums. You can use all-summer fruits or all-winter ones.

**My Most Favorite Sugar Crust (page 108, halving all
the ingredients, except for the egg)**

2 pints blueberries, picked over, rinsed, and dried
2 pints strawberries, hulled, 1 pint sliced and the
other pint halved
¼ cup sugar, or more to taste
1 tablespoon cornstarch
2 tablespoons strawberry preserves
5 large ripe bananas
Juice of ½ lemon
Apricot preserves, melted and still warm, for glaze

1. Preheat the oven to 350 degrees F. Remove the dough from the refrigerator and let it stand at room temperature for 5 to 10 minutes to soften before rolling out. Line a baking sheet with parchment paper.

2. On a lightly floured surface, roll the dough into a round about 11 inches in diameter. Lightly roll the dough over the rolling pin, center the rolling pin over a 10-inch fluted tart pan with a removable bottom, and unroll the dough over the pan. Gently press the dough over the bottom and up the sides of the pan. With a pastry scraper or with the rolling pin, trim the overhang of the dough even with the edge of the pan. Refrigerate the tart shell while you make the filling.

3. In a large bowl, combine 2 cups of the blueberries and the sliced strawberries, sugar, cornstarch, and strawberry preserves. Toss gently, taking care not to crush the berries, until the preserves are well incorporated and coat the fruit. Taste and add additional sugar, if desired. Spread the berry mixture evenly over the bottom of the tart shell. Place the pan on the lined baking sheet.

4. Bake for 50 minutes. (The fruit will bake down and become somewhat jamlike.) Remove the pan from the oven and cool on a wire rack.

5. To finish the tart: Arrange 2 rows of the halved strawberries directly across the middle of the tart. Cut the bananas into thin slices on the diagonal and brush them with lemon juice to prevent discoloring. Arrange 2 rows of the sliced bananas, overlapping the slices slightly, next to the rows of strawberries. Mound blueberries next to the bananas. (The top of the tart should be entirely fruit covered.)

6. With a pastry brush, brush the fruits with the warm apricot preserves, taking care not to disturb the arrangement. Before serving, remove the sides of the tart pan and place the tart on a serving plate. Serve at room temperature. Store leftovers, covered with plastic wrap, in the refrigerator for 1 day.

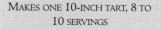

Blueberry Tart

This blueberry tart is not too sweet and has a lovely lift from the grated lemon zest and a little bit of cinnamon in the filling. Be sure to taste the filling before you bake it. If it is not sweet enough, try adding more apricot preserves rather than sugar. The preserves add a hint of fruitiness—almost a perfume—which the sugar cannot.

My Most Favorite Sugar Crust (page 108, halving all
    the ingredients, except for the egg)
3 pints blueberries, picked over, rinsed, and dried
½ cup sugar, or more to taste
1 tablespoon cornstarch
2 tablespoons apricot preserves
¼ teaspoon ground cinnamon
¼ teaspoon freshly grated lemon zest, or to taste
Apricot preserves, melted and still warm, for glaze
    (optional)

I. Preheat the oven to 350 degrees F. Remove the dough from the refrigerator and let it stand at room temperature for 5 to 10 minutes to soften before rolling out. Line a baking sheet with parchment paper.

2. On a lightly floured surface, roll the dough into a round about 11 inches in diameter. Lightly roll the dough over the rolling pin, center the rolling pin over a 10-inch fluted tart pan with a removable bottom, and unroll the dough over the pan. With a pastry scraper or with the rolling pin, trim the overhang of the dough even with the edge of the pan. Refrigerate the tart shell while you make the filling.

3. Make the filling: In a medium bowl, combine 2 pints (4 cups) of the blueberries, sugar, cornstarch, apricot preserves, cinnamon, and lemon zest. Toss together gently, taking care not to crush the berries, until the preserves are incorporated. Taste and add additional preserves or sugar, if desired. Spread the filling evenly over the dough in the tart pan. Place the pan on the lined baking sheet.

4. Bake for 45 to 50 minutes until the filling has baked down and become thickened and jamlike. Remove the tart to a wire rack and let cool completely.

5. To finish the tart: Mound the remaining blueberries over the filling. If desired, with a pastry brush, dab the berries with the apricot glaze to make them glisten. Before serving, remove the sides of the tart pan and place the tart on a serving plate. Serve at room temperature. Store leftovers, covered with plastic wrap, in the refrigerator for 1 day.

Mixed Berry Tart

MAKES ONE 10-INCH TART

As I mentioned before, my daughter Renée is a very fine baker. She loves to entertain, and one summer day decided to put together a tart from the berries she had on hand. This is what she came up with. It is a summer-fruit extravaganza, with strawberries, blueberries, and raspberries. I'm sure she would have used blackberries, too, had she had some that day. If summer could be tasted, this is how it would taste.

My Most Favorite Sugar Crust (page 108, halving all
    the ingredients, except for the egg)

FILLING
1½ cups hulled chopped strawberries
1½ cups blueberries, picked over, rinsed, and dried
1 cup raspberries, rinsed
¼ cup sugar
2 tablespoons flour
2 tablespoons raspberry preserves, with or without
    seeds
Pinch of ground cinnamon (optional)

TOPPING
About 3 cups combined sliced strawberries,
    blueberries, and raspberries

1. Preheat the oven to 375 degrees F. Remove the dough from the refrigerator and let it stand at room temperature for 5 to 10 minutes to soften before rolling out. Line a baking sheet with parchment paper.

2. On a lightly floured surface, roll the dough into a round about 11 inches in diameter. Lightly roll the dough over the rolling pin, center the rolling pin over a 10-inch fluted tart pan with a removable bottom, and unroll the dough over the pan. Gently press the dough over the bottom and up the sides of the pan. With a pastry scraper or with the rolling pin, trim the overhang of the dough even with the edge of the pan. Refrigerate the tart shell while you make the filling.

3. Make the filling: In a medium bowl, combine all the filling ingredients including the cinnamon, if using. Toss together gently, taking care not to crush the berries, until the raspberry preserves are incorporated and the fruit is coated. Taste and add additional sugar and/or preserves, if desired. Spread the filling evenly over the dough in the tart pan. Place the pan on the lined baking sheet.

4. Bake for about 40 to 50 minutes until the filling has baked down and is thickened and jamlike. Remove the pan from the oven and let the tart shell cool on a wire rack.

5. To finish the tart: Mound the combined berries over the filling. Before serving, remove the sides of the pan and place the tart on a serving plate. Serve at room temperature. Store leftovers, covered with plastic wrap, in the refrigerator for 1 day.

Pear Frangipane Tart

I have always loved frangipane, a rich pastry cream flavored with ground almonds. Because I don't make pastry cream at My Most Favorite Dessert Company, I have come up with a frangipane facsimile, which combines almond paste, margarine, and egg. It is a perfect match with pears but can be paired with apples and plums as well. If you like almonds, you will love this rich-tasting tart, so perfect for serving in the fall and winter.

My Most Favorite Sugar Crust for one 10-inch tart
    (page 108, halving all the ingredients, except for
    the egg)

FRANGIPANE MIXTURE
4 tablespoons (½ stick) unsalted margarine
2 tablespoons sugar
1 large egg
6 ounces almond paste

3 firm but ripe large Bartlett or Bosc pears
3 tablespoons apricot preserves
½ tablespoon fresh lemon juice, or to taste

141

1. Preheat the oven to 350 degrees F. Remove the dough from the refrigerator and let it stand at room temperature for 5 to 10 minutes before rolling out. Line a baking sheet with parchment paper.

2. On a lightly floured surface, roll the dough into a round about 11 inches in diameter. Lightly roll the dough over the rolling pin, center the rolling pin over a 10-inch fluted tart pan with a removable bottom, and unroll the dough over the pan. Gently press the dough over the bottom and up the sides of the pan. With a pastry scraper or with the rolling pin, trim the overhang of the dough even with the edge of the pan. Refrigerate the tart shell while you make the filling.

3. Make the frangipane mixture: With a handheld mixer, cream the margarine and sugar in a medium bowl. Add the egg and beat until incorporated. Break the almond paste into the bowl, crumbling it in with your hands, and beat it into the margarine mixture until smooth. Spread in an even layer over the bottom of the tart. Place the tart pan on the lined baking sheet.

4. Halve each pear and remove the core and stem. Cut each half into slices, without detaching them at the top. Arrange the pear halves, skin side up, on the frangipane and, with the palm of your hand, fan the slices out slightly. (The pears should not entirely cover the filling.)

5. Bake the tart for 25 to 35 minutes until the frangipane is nicely browned and the pears are soft when tested. Remove the tart to a wire rack and let it cool completely.

6. In a small saucepan, melt the apricot preserves with the lemon juice, stirring until combined. With a pastry brush, brush just the pears with the apricot glaze. Before serving, remove the sides of the pan and place the tart on a serving plate. Serve at room temperature. Store leftovers, covered with plastic wrap, in the refrigerator for 1 day.

To Ripen Pears

It is very difficult to find ripe pears in the supermarket, the reason being that they are too fragile when ripe not to bruise in transit. What you will find are pears that range from hard to rock-solid. To ripen them so that they can be used, place the pears in a paper bag (along with an apple or a banana), close the bag, and store it at room temperature for 3 to 4 days, sometimes for as long as 5 to 6 days. Ethylene gas, emitted by the apple or banana, serves to move the process along. Be sure to turn the bag to prevent the pears from bruising while they stand. Once ripe, they should be used or refrigerated. Don't think that baking hard pears will soften them enough to be appetizing. It doesn't.

Strawberry Tart
with Crumb Topping

The crunch of a crisp crust, the surprise of a jamlike filling, and a crumbly brown-sugar topping combine to make this a superb summertime dessert. Only lush, ripe strawberries will do.

My Most Favorite Sugar Crust (page 108, halving all the ingredients, except for the egg)

FILLING
3 cups strawberries, hulled, rinsed and dried, and cut into medium pieces
2 tablespoons raspberry preserves, with or without seeds
¼ cup granulated sugar
Pinch of ground cinnamon
4 tablespoons all-purpose flour

CRUMB TOPPING
½ cup all-purpose flour
½ cup firmly packed light brown sugar
1 teaspoon ground cinnamon
4 tablespoons (½ stick) cold unsalted margarine, cut into small pieces

1. Preheat the oven to 375 degrees F. Remove the dough from the refrigerator and let it stand at room temperature for 5 to 10 minutes to soften before rolling out.

2. On a lightly floured surface, roll the dough into a round about 11 inches in diameter. Lightly roll the dough over the rolling pin, center the rolling pin over a 10-inch fluted tart pan with a removable bottom, and unroll the dough over the pan. Gently press the dough over the bottom and up the sides of the pan. With a pastry scraper or with the rolling pin, trim the overhang of the dough even with the edge of the pan. Refrigerate the tart shell while you make the filling and topping.

3. Prepare the filling: In a bowl combine the berries, raspberry preserves, sugar, cinnamon, and flour, mixing well to dissolve the preserves.

4. Make the crumb topping: In a bowl stir together the flour, sugar, and cinnamon until well combined. Add the margarine and rub the mixture between the palms of your hands until it resembles large grains of sand. (It should be finely rubbed; the pieces should not be the size of pebbles.)

5. Remove the tart shell from the refrigerator, fill it with the strawberry filling, spreading it evenly, then top it with the crumb mixture. Place the tart on a baking sheet and bake it for 45 to 50 minutes until the edges are golden and the filling is bubbly.

6. Transfer the tart to a wire rack and let it cool completely. Before serving, remove the sides of the pan and place the tart on a serving plate. Serve. Store leftovers, covered with plastic wrap, in the refrigerator for 1 day.

Lemon Meringue
Tart

This exceptionally beautiful tart should be finished in one serving because the meringue topping does not hold up if stored. Given that this is my favorite tart of all the ones we make, I have no problem with that at all!

Note: The sugar crust can be made in advance; both the lemon filling and meringue should be combined right before you need to use them.

My Most Favorite Sugar Crust (page 108, halving all the ingredients, except for the egg)
1 recipe Lemon Bar filling (page 159)
1 recipe Vanilla Meringues batter (page 232)

1. Preheat the oven to 350 degrees F. Remove the dough from the refrigerator and let it stand at room temperature for 5 to 10 minutes to soften before rolling out.
2. On a lightly floured surface, roll the dough into a round about 11 inches in diameter. Lightly roll the dough over the rolling pin, center the rolling pin over a 10-inch fluted tart pan with a removable bottom, and unroll the dough over the pan. Gently press the dough over the bottom and up the sides of the pan. With a pastry scraper or

with the rolling pin, trim the overhang of the dough even with the edge of the pan. Refrigerate the tart shell briefly.

3. Pour the lemon filling into the lined tart pan, smoothing it into an even layer, if necessary. Bake the tart for about 25 minutes, or until the filling is set. Remove the tart from the oven and let it cool completely on a wire rack. Turn off the oven.

4. When ready to finish the tart, preheat the oven to 500 degrees F.

5. Place the stiffly beaten meringue in a pastry bag fitted with a star tip (Aleco 823). Starting on the outside of the tart, pipe the meringue in about 1-inch-high peaks, proceeding around the tart in concentric circles, until the top is completely covered. (You can also spread it with a spatula, creating little peaks or teardrops, if desired.) Place the tart in the oven for 2 to 3 minutes, checking it frequently, until the meringue peaks are lightly browned. You do not want the meringue to burn.

6. Remove the tart from the oven and let it cool on a wire rack. Before serving, remove the sides of the pan and place the tart on a serving plate. Serve.

Plum Tart

To me, plum tart is the quintessential European pastry—elegant but simple, tart but sweet. This one is especially easy to make and beautiful in its simplicity. If you want to substitute Italian prune plums for a late-summer version of this, halve, pit, and slice them, keeping the end of each half intact. Place each half on the pastry, fanning the slices slightly, until the pastry is covered. Because Italian prune plums are so much smaller than red plums, you will need almost twice the amount: 4 cups of halved Italian prune plums.

My Most Favorite Sugar Crust (page 108, halving all
the ingredients, except for the egg)
3 medium ripe red plums, such as Santa Rosa plums
¹/₄ cup raspberry preserves
¹/₃ cup sugar
Raspberry jelly thinned with splash of kirsch or
1 tablespoon water for glaze

1. Preheat the oven to 325 degrees F. Remove the dough from the refrigerator and let stand at room temperature for 5 to 10 minutes to soften before rolling out.
2. On a lightly floured surface, roll the dough into a round, about 11 inches in diameter. Lightly roll the dough over the rolling pin, center over a 10-inch fluted tart pan with a removable bottom, and unroll

the dough over the pan. Gently press the dough over the bottom and up the sides of the pan. With a pastry scraper or with the rolling pin, trim the overhang of dough, even with the edge of the pan. Refrigerate the shell while you prepare the plums.

3. With a sharp paring knife, halve each plum and remove the pit. Slice each halved plum into wedges ⅛ inch thick. (You will need 2 heaping cups of plum slices.)

4. In a medium bowl, stir the raspberry preserves the sugar until well combined. Add the plum slices and stir gently with a rubber spatula until well coated.

5. Remove the shell from the refrigerator. Starting at the outside edge, arrange the plum slices on their sides in a single layer in concentric circles, covering the pastry shell completely. Place the tart on a baking sheet and bake for about 55 minutes, until the edges are golden. Transfer the tart to a wire rack and let stand while you prepare the glaze.

6. Place the raspberry jelly mixture in a small saucepan and warm it over medium heat, stirring, until slightly thickened. With a pastry brush, brush the glaze lightly over the plum slices, careful not to disturb the design. When ready to serve, remove the side of the tart pan and place the tart on a serving platter. The tart is best if served the same day because the plum slices can make the crust soggy. Leftovers should be stored in the refrigerator.

Cookies

BAR COOKIES

My Most Favorite Brownies

Luscious Lemon Bars

Apricot Meringue Bars

Pecan Diamonds

ASSORTED DROP, CUTOUT, AND SHAPED
COOKIES, PLUS MERINGUES

Chocolate Chocolate Chip Cookies

Peanut Butter Cookies

Old-Fashioned Vanilla Wafers

Chocolate and Hazelnut Biscotti

Chocolate Chip Sand Tarts

My Most Favorite Sugar Cookies

Linzer Cookies

Hamantaschen

Rugelach

Teiglach

Jelly Doughnuts

Vanilla Crescent Cookies

Viennese Nut Cookies

Viennese Orange Cookies

Chocolate Délices

Pecan Délices

Introduction

This chapter is a collection of my most favorite cookies. They range from the simplest drop cookies, to a wonderful peanut butter creation, to elegant Linzer cutouts. Years ago, when I adapted these recipes to pareve, the cookie category presented the least number of challenges from a technical point of view. Many of the cookies we enjoy daily are not made with butter in the first place, and on the occasion when butter was the original ingredient, margarine was often (not always, I admit) an undetectable substitute.

You will find holiday specialties here: Hamentaschen, Teiglach, and Jelly Doughnuts. Still more cookie recipes appear in Passover Baking, on page 201, including Vanilla and Chocolate Meringues, Coconut Macaroons, and a handful of drop cookies made with matzo cake meal. And while my signature brownies are in this chapter, you'll find an equally wonderful recipe for Passover Brownies on page 228.

I was born in Vienna, and my bias for all things baked Viennese style shows in this chapter. There are three different ways to make Linzer Cookies; there's a recipe for Viennese Nut Cookies, followed by one for Orange Cookies, also from Vienna. What all these Viennese recipes have in common is elegance and sophistication, a delicateness that I love. They are the cookies you could imagine yourself having with coffee at a *Konditorei* off the Stephensplatz in the afternoon.

Bar Cookies

My Most Favorite Brownies

There are several signature desserts at My Most Favorite Dessert Company, and one of them is brownies. No one makes a pareve brownie that even comes close to these. Our customers always ask what makes them so good. I think it is the pure chocolate and the addition of chocolate chips that make them especially gooey, chewy, and rich, a little like candy bars. They also stand higher than regular brownies, which adds to their appeal. Make sure to use the best-quality chocolate you can. I use Bloomer's chocolate, which I buy wholesale.

This is exactly how we make them, right down to the pan size. Since some people like to bake brownies in a square pan, the directions appear in the Note. Brownies freeze beautifully. A Little Piece of Advice on page 158 tells you how to freeze the brownies. If you ever need a quick chocolate fix, a frozen brownie is the way to go.

MAKES ONE 11½ × 7½-INCH
PAN OF BROWNIES

1 cup all-purpose flour
⅛ teaspoon baking soda
Pinch of salt
½ pound (2 sticks) unsalted margarine, cut into
    pieces
4 ounces semisweet chocolate, coarsely chopped
2 cups sugar
3 extra-large eggs
2 teaspoons pure vanilla extract
¾ cup miniature semisweet chocolate chips
¾ cup chopped walnuts (optional)

A Little Piece of Advice: You can never have enough of anything baked with chocolate—cakes, cookies, brownies. That's why I always have a batch or two of brownies on hand—in the freezer. They freeze beautifully.

Let the brownies cool completely. Then place the pan, uncovered, in the freezer and let the brownies freeze until solid. Cover the pan with plastic wrap and slide it into a Ziploc freezer bag. Bag it a second time. Return the pan to the freezer and freeze for up to 3 months.

To thaw: Remove the pan from the freezer and uncover completely. Let stand at room temperature until ready to serve.

1. Preheat the oven to 350 degrees F. Grease an 11½ × 7½-inch baking pan.

2. In a bowl combine the flour, baking soda, and salt, stirring to blend.

3. In the top of a double boiler set over hot water, combine the margarine and coarsely chopped semisweet chocolate. Heat, stirring occasionally, until melted and shiny. Remove the pan from the heat, remove the top of the double boiler, and let the mixture cool to room temperature, stirring occasionally.

4. In the bowl of a standing electric mixer fitted with the paddle attachment, combine the sugar, eggs, and cooled chocolate mixture. Beat on medium speed until well mixed. Blend in the vanilla.

5. Turn off the mixer, add all the dry ingredients at one time, and blend on low speed until incorporated. Scrape down the sides of the bowl with a rubber spatula and stir in the chocolate chips and the optional nuts.

6. Scrape the batter into the prepared pan, and level the top. Bake for 35 minutes for fudgy brownies—a cake tester inserted in the center of one will come out with some batter on it. Do not overbake. Remove the pan from the oven to a wire rack and let it cool slightly. These brownies are fantastic served while still warm, and they are just as good at room temperature. Keep, covered with plastic wrap, in the refrigerator for up to 4 days, or freeze as directed in A Little Piece of Advice.

Luscious Lemon Bars

MAKES ONE 11½ × 7½-INCH PAN, OR ABOUT 24 SMALL BARS

I would be very surprised if you have ever tasted lemon bars like these. Instead of using a short sugar crust for the base, we used our Linzer Cookie dough. The combination of the rich almond dough and the slightly tart lemon filling is unique. If you prefer a crust without nuts, use the sugar crust on page 108 as the base.

1 recipe Linzer Cookie dough (page 177)

FILLING
3 extra-large eggs
1 cup granulated sugar
½ cup fresh lemon juice, strained
1 tablespoon freshly grated lemon zest
3 level tablespoons flour
¾ teaspoon baking powder
Pinch of salt

Confectioners' sugar, for dusting

1. Preheat the oven to 350 degrees F.
2. On a lightly floured surface, roll the dough into a 12 × 8-inch rectangle. Gently roll the dough over the rolling pin, center the pin

159

over an $11\frac{1}{2} \times 7\frac{1}{2}$-inch baking pan, and unroll the dough over the pan. Press the dough gently over the bottom and up the sides of the pan. Fold the overhang in to form a slightly higher edge all the way around the pan.

3. Make the filling: In the bowl of a standing electric mixer fitted with the paddle attachment, beat the eggs together very well. Add the sugar and beat until blended. Add the remaining filling ingredients and beat just until combined. Do not overbeat.

4. Pour the filling into the lined baking pan and bake for 20 to 25 minutes (the filling will turn slightly golden on the top). Remove the pan from the oven and cool it completely on a wire rack. Invert the pastry onto a serving plate, and invert it again to set it right side up. Dust generously with confectioners' sugar and cut into bars or squares to serve. The lemon bars keep, covered with plastic wrap, in the refrigerator for 3 days.

Apricot
Meringue Bars

MAKES ONE 13 × 9 × 2-INCH
PAN OF BARS

If I had to list favorite ingredients in order of preference, chocolate would definitely appear at the head of the list, followed by almost any dessert made with lemon or apricot. Here apricot preserves serve as a thin but noticeable layer, separating a nutty meringue from a bar-cookie crust. The pleasure lies in how the different flavors and textures play off each other. Raspberry preserves could be used instead of the apricot here, as could a rough-cut marmalade.

1 cup all-purpose flour
$\frac{1}{2}$ teaspoon salt
$\frac{1}{4}$ teaspoon baking soda
8 tablespoons (1 stick) unsalted margarine
$\frac{1}{2}$ cup plus $\frac{1}{4}$ cup sugar
1 teaspoon freshly grated lemon zest
2 extra-large eggs, separated
$1\frac{1}{2}$ cups apricot preserves
$\frac{1}{2}$ cup finely chopped walnuts

1. Preheat the oven to 350 degrees F. Grease a 13 × 9 × 2-inch baking pan.
2. In a bowl stir together the flour, salt, and baking soda.

3. In the bowl of a standing electric mixer fitted with the paddle attachment, cream the margarine and ½ cup sugar on medium speed until fluffy. Stir in the lemon zest.

4. Add the egg yolks, I at a time, beating well after each addition.

5. Turn off the machine and add the dry ingredients. Beat on low speed until a dough forms around the paddle. Gently press the dough over the bottom of the greased pan.

6. With a metal spatula, spread the apricot preserves evenly over the dough.

7. Wash out the bowl of the mixer, dry it well, and fit the machine with the whisk attachment. Add the egg whites and beat on high speed until foamy. Gradually add ¼ cup sugar and beat until the meringue holds stiff peaks. Fold in the chopped walnuts. Spread the meringue over the apricot preserves.

8. Bake for 30 to 35 minutes until the meringue topping is lightly browned. Remove the pan from the oven and let it cool before cutting into bars. Store the bars, covered with plastic wrap, at room temperature for up to 3 days.

Pecan Diamonds

&

We use the same filling in these bar cookies as in Pecan Pie (page 130)—with two significant differences: We use more of it, and more pecans as well! If you are thinking these bars might not be rich enough, or nutty enough, think again. They are beyond rich. This is one instance where a *small* diamond is best.

My Most Favorite Sugar Crust for one 10-inch crust (page 108)

FILLING
4 tablespoons (½ stick) unsalted margarine
1¼ cups light Karo syrup
1 cup sugar
½ teaspoon salt
3 extra-large eggs, lightly beaten
1 teaspoon pure vanilla extract
1½ cups pecan pieces

1. Preheat the oven to 350 degrees F.
2. On a lightly floured surface, roll the dough into a 10-inch square. Gently roll the dough over the rolling pin, center it over a 9-inch

MAKES ONE 9-INCH PAN OF COOKIES, ABOUT 24 DIAMONDS

square baking pan, and unroll the dough over the pan. Press the dough gently over the bottom and up the sides of the baking pan. Trim the overhang with the top edge of the pan, then with your fingers press it down about ¼ inch from the top. Discard the dough trimmings.

3. Make the filling following the directions on page 131 for Pecan Pie. Add the pecans and stir well to combine.

4. Pour the filling into the lined baking pan and, if necessary, evenly distribute the pecans. (The filling should come right up to the top edge of the dough.) Bake for 45 to 55 minutes until the filling is just set. Remove the pan to a wire rack and let it cool completely before cutting into slender bars or small diamond shapes. Store the bars, covered with plastic wrap, in the refrigerator for up to 4 days.

Assorted Drop, Cutout, and Shaped Cookies, Plus Meringues

Chocolate Chocolate Chip Cookies

These cookies are loaded with chocolate. They are also bite-size, which means you get less in one bite, but I've never known anyone who could stop at just one.

¾ cup all-purpose flour
⅓ cup unsweetened cocoa powder
1 teaspoon baking powder
½ teaspoon salt
8 tablespoons (1 stick) unsalted margarine, at room temperature
½ cup firmly packed light brown sugar
½ cup granulated sugar
1 extra-large egg, at room temperature
1 teaspoon pure vanilla extract
1¼ cups (9 ounces) regular-size semisweet chocolate chips

1. Preheat the oven to 350 degrees F. Line 2 large baking sheets with parchment paper.
2. In a medium bowl, sift together the flour, cocoa, baking powder, and salt.

3. In the bowl of an electric mixer fitted with the paddle attachment, cream the margarine until soft. Add the brown and white sugars gradually, beating on low speed until smooth. Beat in the egg until combined. Stir in the dry ingredients until incorporated. Add the vanilla and the chocolate chips, stirring until combined.

4. Drop the batter by teaspoonfuls onto the prepared baking sheets, leaving about 2 inches between each. Bake the cookies 10 to 12 minutes until they just feel firm on top. Do not overbake. Transfer the baking sheets to cooling racks and let the cookies cool for about 5 minutes. Remove the cookies to the racks to cool completely. Store, in layers, in airtight containers for up to 1 week. Or freeze them in a freezer plastic bag for up to 1 month.

Peanut Butter Cookies

MAKES ABOUT 3 DOZEN COOKIES, EACH 2½ TO 3 INCHES IN DIAMETER

These cookies are for all dedicated peanut butter lovers. My friend Henry said that not even his mother's peanut butter cookies, which have been a family favorite for years, rival them. What makes them especially wonderful are the chunks of semisweet chocolate—I am not talking chips here—that you get in each bite. Like Chocolate Chocolate Chip Cookies (page 166), these are divine served warm, while the chocolate is still soft.

1½ cups all-purpose flour
1 teaspoon baking soda
½ teaspoon baking powder
¼ teaspoon salt
8 tablespoons (1 stick) unsalted margarine, at room temperature
½ cup granulated sugar
½ cup firmly packed light brown sugar
2 extra-large eggs
¾ cup smooth peanut butter
3 tablespoons fresh orange juice
1 teaspoon pure vanilla extract
1½ cups chopped semisweet chocolate

1. Preheat the oven to 375 degrees F. Line 2 large baking sheets with parchment paper.

2. In a large bowl, stir together the flour, baking soda, baking powder, and salt until combined.

3. In the bowl of an electric mixer fitted with the paddle attachment, cream together the margarine and the white and brown sugars on low speed until fluffy. Beat in the eggs until incorporated, then beat in the peanut butter. Scrape down the sides of the bowl and stir in the orange juice and the vanilla.

4. Still on low speed, beat in the dry ingredients until combined. By hand, stir in the chopped chocolate until the pieces are well distributed.

5. Drop the dough by *heaping*, really rounded tablespoons onto the prepared baking sheets, leaving 2 inches between the mounds. Bake on the middle rack of the oven, rotating the sheets halfway through the baking time, for 10 to 12 minutes until lightly colored on the top and bottom. Transfer the cookies with a metal spatula to wire racks to cool. If you have any of these left over, store them in an airtight container in a secret place!

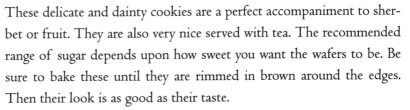

Old-Fashioned
Vanilla Wafers

MAKES ABOUT 4 DOZEN 2-INCH
WAFERS

These delicate and dainty cookies are a perfect accompaniment to sherbet or fruit. They are also very nice served with tea. The recommended range of sugar depends upon how sweet you want the wafers to be. Be sure to bake these until they are rimmed in brown around the edges. Then their look is as good as their taste.

Cake flour renders a tender cookie. If you do not have any, you can substitute all-purpose flour, with a slight adjustment. Sift it first as directed, then remove a scant 2 teaspoons from the measurement.

8 tablespoons (1 stick) unsalted margarine, at room
  temperature
⅓ to ½ cup sugar
1 extra-large egg
1 teaspoon pure vanilla extract
1 teaspoon finely grated orange zest
¼ teaspoon finely grated lemon zest
¾ cup sifted cake flour

1. Preheat the oven to 375 degrees F. Line 2 large baking sheets with parchment paper.
2. In the bowl of an electric mixer fitted with the paddle attachment, cream the margarine together with the sugar on low speed until

fluffy. Scrape down the bowl with a rubber spatula, then beat in the egg and vanilla until incorporated. Stir in the orange and lemon zests.

3. Still on low speed, beat in the flour until fully blended.

4. By teaspoonfuls, drop the batter onto the prepared baking sheets, leaving a good 2 inches between each. Bake the cookies, rotating the sheets halfway through the baking time, for a total of about 7 minutes, or until the wafers are lightly browned around the edges. With a metal spatula, transfer the wafers to cooling racks, where they will crisp as they cool. Store carefully, in layers, in an airtight container for up to 1 week.

Chocolate and Hazelnut Biscotti

MAKES 2 DOZEN BISCOTTI

My daughter Renée and I give cooking demonstrations for people who keep kosher homes. We often make these biscotti, which students believe are difficult to make until they see it done. Renée explains that just because biscotti are twice baked doesn't mean they are complicated. Try these: The combination of hazelnuts and chocolate makes them particularly appealing.

1¾ cups all-purpose flour
½ teaspoon baking powder
Pinch of salt
3 extra-large whole eggs, at room temperature
1 extra-large egg yolk, at room temperature
1 cup sugar
1 teaspoon pure vanilla extract
1 cup chopped bittersweet chocolate (medium-size chunks)
2 cups hazelnuts, toasted and skinned (see opposite), coarsely chopped

1. Preheat the oven to 350 degrees F. Grease 2 large cookie sheets.
2. Place the flour, baking powder, and salt in a large bowl; stir to combine.

3. In the bowl of a standing electric mixer fitted with the paddle attachment, combine 2 of the whole eggs, the egg yolk, and the sugar and beat on medium speed until well blended.

4. Add the dry ingredients, a little at a time, and beat until well combined. By hand, fold in the chocolate and the chopped hazelnuts.

5. On a lightly floured surface, knead the dough until smooth, about 3 minutes. Divide the dough in half and shape each half into a log, 12 inches long and 2½ inches wide. Place 1 log on each of the cookie sheets. Beat the remaining egg to make an egg wash, and brush each of the logs with egg wash. Bake the loaves for 35 minutes.

6. Remove the cookie sheets from the oven and reduce the oven temperature to 325 degrees F.

7. With a sharp knife, cut each log crosswise into 1-inch slices. Lay the slices, cut side down, on each baking sheet.

8. Return the sheets to the oven and bake the biscotti for 15 minutes. Let cool on the sheets on wire racks. Store in airtight containers where they will keep for at least 1 week.

To Toast and Skin Hazelnuts

Spread the hazelnuts out on a baking sheet and toast them in a preheated 350 degree F oven, stirring once or twice, for about 15 minutes, or until the skins blister. Wrap the hot nuts in a clean kitchen towel, let stand for a few minutes to steam, then, still wrapped in the towel, rub them against each other to remove the skins. Not every last piece will come off, but a piece of skin here and there is all right. You do not want a lot to remain, however, because it tastes bitter.

Chocolate Chip
Sand Tarts

I don't remember how these cookies came to be called sand tarts. They're not tarts at all, but tender, crumbly, almost shortbread-type cookies in the shape of a heart. They are delicate and fanciful, and exquisitely rich, not just because of the margarine and sugar in the dough, but because they contain a good amount of ground pecans as well. When my son Philip was in high school, he and a group of friends would come over to our house after school. I would put a big bowl of these, freshly baked, out on the counter. I'd turn around and they'd be gone—six dozen in the blink of an eye!

2¾ cups all-purpose flour
1¼ cups very finely ground pecans
½ pound (2 sticks) unsalted margarine
½ cup sugar plus additional sugar for sprinkling on
    the cookies
1 extra-large egg
1 teaspoon pure vanilla extract
½ cup miniature semisweet chocolate chips

1. Preheat the oven to 350 degrees F. Line 2 large baking sheets with parchment paper.

2. In a bowl stir together the flour and the pecans.

3. In the bowl of a standing electric mixer fitted with the paddle attachment, cream the margarine and the sugar on medium speed until fluffy. Beat in the egg, then the vanilla.

4. Add the dry ingredients, a little at a time, and blend until a dough comes together. Add the chocolate chips and beat just until incorporated.

5. On a lightly floured surface, roll out the dough ¼ inch thick. With a 2-inch-wide heart-shaped cookie cutter, cut out cookies. Place them, about 1 inch apart, on the lined baking sheets. Reroll the scraps and cut out cookies in the same manner. Sprinkle them generously with granulated sugar.

6. Bake the cookies for about 12 minutes, or until just firm to the touch. Remove the baking sheets from the oven to wire racks and let cool for about 5 minutes before removing the cookies to the racks to cool completely. Store, in layers, in airtight containers for up to 1 week.

My Most Favorite
Sugar Cookies

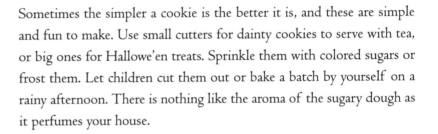

MAKES ABOUT 3 DOZEN 2-INCH
ROUND COOKIES

Sometimes the simpler a cookie is the better it is, and these are simple and fun to make. Use small cutters for dainty cookies to serve with tea, or big ones for Hallowe'en treats. Sprinkle them with colored sugars or frost them. Let children cut them out or bake a batch by yourself on a rainy afternoon. There is nothing like the aroma of the sugary dough as it perfumes your house.

**1 recipe My Most Favorite Sugar Crust (page 108)
Granulated sugar, for sprinkling**

1. Preheat the oven to 350 degrees F. Line 2 large cookie sheets with parchment paper.
2. Let the dough stand at room temperature to soften slightly before rolling. On a lightly floured surface, roll out the dough a generous ¼ inch thick. With your favorite cookie cutters, cut out cookies and place them, 1 inch apart, on the lined sheets. Sprinkle generously with granulated sugar. Gather up the scraps, reroll the dough, cut out, and sugar cookies until you have used up all the dough.
3. Bake for 10 to 12 minutes until just golden on the bottom. With a metal spatula, transfer to wire racks to cool. Store, in layers, in airtight containers for up to 1 week.

Linzer Cookies

MAKES 1 DOZEN COOKIES

When I baked my first Viennese Linzertorte (page 85), I could not believe how beautiful it was. I feel exactly the same way about these Linzer cookies. They are like little jewels, with their ruby centers of raspberry preserves. You can also fill them with apricot jam, which is equally pretty. The almond dough is short, meaning it is rich, and it is sweet and melts in your mouth. These cookies are among my all-time favorites.

  1 cup all-purpose flour
  Large pinch of ground cinnamon
  8 tablespoons (1 stick) unsalted margarine
  1/4 cup granulated sugar
  3/4 cup finely ground unblanched almonds
  Raspberry preserves, with or without seeds
  Confectioners' sugar, for dusting

1. In a bowl stir together the flour and cinnamon.
2. In the bowl of a standing electric mixer fitted with the paddle attachment, cream the margarine and the granulated sugar on medium speed until fluffy.
3. Gradually add the flour mixture and beat on low speed until the

dough comes together in a ball. Add the ground almonds and beat until incorporated. Scrape down the sides of the bowl, shape the dough into a disk, and wrap it in plastic wrap. Refrigerate for several hours until firm enough to roll out.

4. Preheat the oven to 350 degrees F. Line a large baking sheet with parchment paper.

5. On a lightly floured surface, roll out the dough ¼ inch thick. With a 2¼-inch fluted cookie cutter, cut out rounds and place them about 1 inch apart on the prepared baking sheet. Reroll the scraps and cut out more cookies. (When done, you should have about 24 cutouts in all.) Cut out the center of half the cookies, 12 of them, using the wide end of a ¾-inch-wide pastry bag tip. They will be the "top" cookies. Discard the little bits of cutout dough.

6. Bake the cookies for about 12 minutes, or until fragrant and just set. Remove the baking sheet to a wire rack and let cool.

7. To assemble: Sprinkle the cutout (top) 12 cookies generously with confectioners' sugar and reserve. Place a level teaspoon of raspberry preserves on each of the bottom cookies. Place a sugared cutout on top. Store, in a single layer, in an airtight container for up to 1 week, if you are lucky enough to have them for that long.

V A R I A T I O N S

Chocolate-Drizzled Apricot Linzer Cookies

Make the cookies as directed, but do not sprinkle the cooled top cookies with confectioners' sugar. Sandwich the cookies with apricot preserves, ½ teaspoon per cookie. Place the cookies on a parchment paper–lined baking sheet. Using a paper piping cone (see page 70 for instructions on how to make one) or a fork, drizzle melted semisweet

chocolate in a zigzag design over the cookies. Let the chocolate set before serving or storing.

Chocolate-Dipped Linzer Cookies

Make the dough as directed, but roll it out a *scant* ¼ inch thick. Cut into rounds with a 2½-inch round cookie cutter and place on a parchment paper–lined baking sheet. (Do not make cutouts in the centers of any of the cookies.) Bake for 12 to 13 minutes and cool as directed for Linzer Cookies. Sandwich the cookies together with a thin layer of raspberry preserves, ¼ to ½ teaspoon per cookie. Melt 2 ounces semi-sweet chocolate; it should be warm not hot. Dip the top of each cookie into the chocolate, tipping it to cover the sides and top edge completely, then place the cookie, chocolate side up, on a rack set over a baking sheet. Let the chocolate set, about 30 minutes in a cool place, before serving or storing.

MAKES ABOUT 40 PASTRIES

PURIM

The spring holiday of Purim joyously celebrates the downfall of the tyrant Haman, who intended to kill all the Jews in the land of Persia. Queen Esther, a Jewess, intervened on her people's behalf, saving the day. The hamantaschen pastries that we enjoy on this holiday are triangular in shape, symbolic of the three-cornered hat Haman is believed to have worn. On Purim it is traditional to deliver gifts, *mishloah manot*, baskets of food or presents, to family and friends. Typically, included among the gifts are hamantaschen.

Hamantaschen

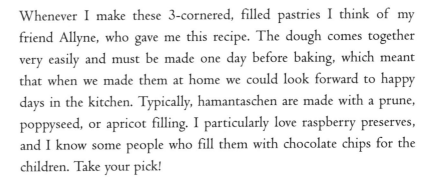

Whenever I make these 3-cornered, filled pastries I think of my friend Allyne, who gave me this recipe. The dough comes together very easily and must be made one day before baking, which meant that when we made them at home we could look forward to happy days in the kitchen. Typically, hamantaschen are made with a prune, poppyseed, or apricot filling. I particularly love raspberry preserves, and I know some people who fill them with chocolate chips for the children. Take your pick!

> 3½ cups all-purpose flour
> 2½ teaspoons baking powder
> 1 cup sugar
> ⅓ cup vegetable oil
> 2 extra-large eggs
> Grated zest of ½ orange
> Grated zest of ½ lemon
> ¼ cup fresh orange juice
> Prune or poppyseed filling; raspberry, strawberry, or
>   apricot preserves; or chocolate chips for filling
> Egg wash of 2 large egg yolks

1. Preheat the oven to 350 degrees F. Line a large baking sheet with parchment paper.

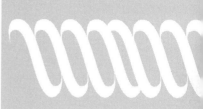

2. In a large bowl, stir together the flour and the baking powder.

3. In the bowl of a standing electric mixer fitted with the paddle attachment, beat the sugar and the vegetable oil on medium speed until combined. Add the eggs and beat until incorporated. Stir in the orange and lemon zests.

4. Reduce the mixer speed to low and add the dry ingredients, alternating with the orange juice, until a dough forms. Shape the dough into a flat disk, wrap it in plastic wrap, and refrigerate it overnight.

5. The next day, remove the dough from the refrigerator and let it stand at room temperature to soften slightly.

6. On a lightly floured surface, roll the dough into a rectangle ¼ inch thick. With a 2¼-inch round fluted cutter, cut out rounds and place them about ½ inch apart on the prepared baking sheet. Reroll the scraps of dough and cut out more rounds. (You should have about 40 rounds of dough.)

7. Place the filling of choice, not the chocolate chips, in a pastry bag fitted with a small plain tip, if desired; or use a small spoon. Place about 1 scant teaspoon of the filling in the center of each round. If using chocolate chips, use about ½ teaspoon per round.

8. Beat the egg yolks together to blend. With a small pastry brush, brush the edges of the rounds lightly with the beaten yolks. Using your thumb and the index finger on each hand, shape each dough round into a triangle, lifting the dough up around the filling. With your thumb and index finger, then press the corners of the 2 sides closest to you to seal, making 2 points of a triangle. Press the third, or remaining, point to seal. You should have 3 points or "corners" on each pastry when done—like a 3-cornered hat.

9. Bake the pastries for about 10 minutes, or until golden brown. Remove the baking sheet to a wire rack and let the pastries cool completely before serving. Store the pastries in an airtight container at room temperature.

TO FREEZE

Place the pastries in a freezer bag and store in the freezer for 2 weeks.

TO DEFROST

Remove the pastries from the plastic freezer bag and let them thaw at room temperature.

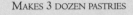

Rugelach

Years ago this recipe was given to me by a Viennese woman. After reading and rereading the recipe, I finally realized that it was for rugelach. I am always eager to try something new and loved this version of rugelach the moment I tasted it. At my bakery in Great Neck, I was amazed at how many rugelach we sold for Rosh Hashanah, in particular. They are clearly a holiday favorite, which has now evolved into a year-round one, judging from their widespread availability.

This is one of the few recipes in this book that calls for nondairy creamer, which came about as a consequence of trying to duplicate the Viennese recipe. Only nondairy creamer seemed to be able to do that. The dough is tender and, when rolled into the horns, has a most beautiful handmade quality. Although rugelach are often filled with apricot preserves, I prefer to use raspberry preserves.

DOUGH
½ pound (2 sticks) unsalted margarine, cut into
    pieces
4 extra-large egg yolks
3 tablespoons nondairy creamer
2½ cups lightly packed all-purpose flour

FILLING

1 cup raspberry preserves, with or without seeds
Cinnamon sugar, made by stirring 1 cup sugar
    together with 1 tablespoon ground cinnamon
3/4 cup finely ground unblanched almonds
1/2 to 3/4 cup dark raisins, or to taste

Egg wash of 1 extra-large egg white, lightly beaten

1. Make the dough: In the bowl of a standing electric mixer fitted with the paddle attachment, cream the margarine on medium speed until fluffy.
2. Add the egg yolks, all at one time, and beat until incorporated.
3. Mix in the nondairy creamer until blended. Scrape down the sides of the bowl with a rubber spatula.
4. Reduce the mixer speed to low and start adding the flour, a little at a time. The dough will begin to form around the paddle. Scrape down the sides of the bowl and continue to add flour, beating on low speed until the dough comes together in a ball.
5. Remove the dough from the bowl, shape it into a disk, and wrap it in plastic wrap. Place the dough in the freezer for 1 hour or in the refrigerator for several hours until firm.
6. Preheat the oven to 350 degrees F. Line 2 large baking sheets with parchment paper.
7. Unwrap the chilled dough and divide it into 3 equal pieces. Working with 1 piece at a time, roll it out on a lightly floured surface into a 10-inch circle, about 1/8 inch thick.
8. Make the filling: Using a metal spatula, spread a third of the raspberry preserves over the dough in a thin layer, leaving a 1/4-inch edge. Sprinkle a scant 2 tablespoons of the cinnamon sugar over the preserves, and top it with a scant 1/4 cup finely ground almonds. Scatter

a scant ¼ cup raisins on top. With the flat side of a long metal spatula, press the filling ingredients lightly onto the dough to adhere.

9. With a pastry cutter or pizza cutter, cut the dough round into 12 equal wedges as you would a pie. Starting at the outside edge (the wide portion of the wedge), roll it firmly toward the center of the round, forming it into a tapering cylinder. (As you roll these, some of the raisins may pop out the sides of the cylinder because not all of them will fit into the tapering shape.) Press the tip of the dough firmly underneath to seal and place the cylinder, tip side down, on one of the lined baking sheets. Continue to roll the rugelach in the same manner, placing them about 2 inches apart, always tip side down, on the baking sheet. Repeat with the remaining pieces of dough and filling ingredients.

10. Brush each of the rugelach with some of the egg wash and sprinkle generously with the remaining cinnamon sugar.

11. Bake the rugelach for 17 to 20 minutes until the tops are golden brown and the dough is baked all the way through. Remove the baking sheets from the oven and let the rugelach stand on the sheets for 5 minutes. Remove the rugelach to wire racks to cool. Store in an airtight container and keep at room temperature for 24 hours. If storing them longer, transfer the rugelach to a freezer plastic bag and store in the refrigerator for several days.

Note: Rugelach can be frozen unbaked. Place the unbaked pastries on a baking sheet and put the sheet in the freezer until the rugelach are frozen solid. Transfer the frozen pastries to a freezer bag and freeze for up to 1 month. To bake: Place the frozen rugelach on a baking sheet and bake at 350 degrees F for about 20 minutes.

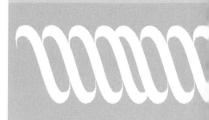

Teiglach

When we lived in King's Point my neighbor Sarah made teiglach on Rosh Hashanah. The honey in the syrup surrounding the dough balls is symbolic of sweetness, and the round shape of the balls themselves reminds one of the hoped-for fullness of the coming new year. Sarah always served these "honey nuts" for dessert. Another friend of mine likes to dip them in hot tea.

I have never seen another recipe for teiglach like this one. The dough is first cooked on the stovetop, *then* baked in the oven.

MAKES 4 TO 6 SERVINGS

1 pound honey
1 cup sugar
1 cup water plus ¼ cup boiling water
4 extra-large eggs, beaten together lightly
1½ cups all-purpose flour
2 cups walnut pieces

1. Preheat the oven to 300 degrees F.
2. In a large heavy ovenproof saucepan, combine the honey, sugar, and 1 cup water and cook over medium-low heat, stirring, until the sugar melts and the mixture is thoroughly blended. Bring the syrup slowly to a boil.
3. Meanwhile, in a large bowl, combine the eggs and the flour and stir until the mixture comes together into a ball of dough. Shape into a

round, then cut it into 6 equal balls. On a floured surface, roll each ball into a rope about 5 inches long. Cut each rope into ½-inch-long pieces.

4. When the honey syrup comes to a boil, add the dough pieces to the pan and cook for 5 minutes. Cover, transfer the pan to the middle rack of the oven, and bake for 25 minutes.

5. Add the walnuts to the pan and bake for 25 minutes more. Remove the pan from the oven and stir in ¼ cup boiling water. Pour the mixture into a large heatproof serving dish and let cool. Serve in dessert bowls and recommend that guests pull the dough balls off with their fingers.

ROSH HASHANAH

Rosh Hashanah is the Jewish New Year and celebrates the beginning of the world. The holiday takes place in September or early October. Jews pray for a sweet year to come. The foods of Rosh Hashanah should be sweet only, nothing sour—apples, honey, sweet wine. Traditionally, we dip apples in honey, symbolic of the hope that sweetness will prevail over the course of the year. The desserts associated with Rosh Hashanah are honey cake, Honey Apple Cake (see page 36 for my variation), and teiglach—all sweet, all with honey.

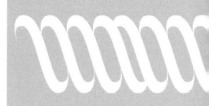

Jelly Doughnuts

Hanukkah celebratory foods always include oil, which commemorates the sacred oil used in the menorah that lit the Temple after its recapture by Judah Maccabaeus. On Hanukkah many Eastern European Jews make potato latkes and fry them in oil. Jelly doughnuts, also fried, are traditional for Hanukkah among Sephardim. I learned about these doughnuts from my first baker in Great Neck, who was an Israeli from Morocco. There are two keys to their success: Be generous with the amount of jelly (preserves in my recipe) and serve the doughnuts as soon as they are made. The fresher they are, the better.

DOUGH
2½ cups all-purpose flour
¼ teaspoon salt
½ ounce cake yeast
½ cup vanilla soy milk (see headnote, page 26)
2 extra-large egg yolks
1 whole extra-large egg
2 tablespoons granulated sugar
4 tablespoons (½ stick) unsalted margarine
Finely grated zest and the juice of ½ lemon

(ingredients continued)

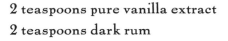

2 teaspoons pure vanilla extract
2 teaspoons dark rum

Vegetable oil, for deep frying
Strawberry or raspberry preserves, for filling
Confectioners' sugar, for dusting

1. Make the dough: In a medium bowl, stir together the flour and the salt. Flour a sheet pan or large baking sheet.

2. In the bowl of a standing electric mixer fitted with the dough hook, combine all the ingredients for the dough, adding the flour mixture last. Turn the machine on to medium speed and beat the mixture until it forms a dough and comes together in a ball around the hook. Continue to beat the dough until it cleans the sides of the bowl. Remove the dough to the floured sheet pan, spread it out in an even layer, dust it lightly with flour, and cover the pan well with plastic wrap. Store it in the refrigerator overnight.

3. The next day, lightly flour a large work surface. Roll the dough into a large rectangle about ¼ inch thick. Let the rolled-out dough relax on the work surface for 3 to 4 minutes. (It will shrink in size slightly.)

4. While the dough is resting, cover 2 large baking sheets each with a clean kitchen towel. Flour the towels lightly.

5. With a 2½-inch round cutter, cut out rounds of dough and place them about 2 inches apart on the baking sheets. Gather together the scraps, reroll, let rest, and cut out more rounds until you have used all the dough. Do not cover the rounds on the baking sheets.

6. Transfer the baking sheets to a warm, draft-free place and let the doughnuts rise until almost double in size, puffed, and very soft to the touch. (How long will depend upon the temperature of your kitchen, but you should allow 3 to 4 hours for the dough to rise.)

7. When the doughnuts have just about doubled in size, place a large saucepan on the stove. Pour about 3 inches of vegetable oil into the pan and heat it over medium heat until it registers 350 degrees F on a deep-fry thermometer. Be careful not to overheat the oil. Place a few doughnuts at a time carefully in the hot oil and deep-fry them, turning them with a skimmer, until golden. If your oil is the right temperature, this should take 4 to 5 minutes. Transfer them with a skimmer to paper towels to drain. Check the temperature of the oil and continue to deep-fry doughnuts with the remaining dough in the same way, being sure to add the pieces carefully to the hot oil.

8. Fill and sugar the doughnuts: Fill a pastry bag fitted with a plain tip with strawberry or raspberry preserves. Make a small hole in the side of each doughnut and pipe the preserves into the middle. Be generous with the amount of filling. Dust the doughnuts with confectioners' sugar, place them on a serving platter, and serve at once.

HANUKKAH

The holiday of Hanukkah commemorates the legend of the oil. When Judah Maccabaeus recaptured the Temple in Jerusalem in 165 B.C.E., he found one jar of oil, enough to burn for only one day. That oil, miraculously, lasted for eight days, hence the tradition of lighting the menorah, from the Hebrew word meaning candlestick, on eight successive nights. The word *Hanukkah* means "dedication": Because of the light, Jews were able once again to worship in the Temple.

Hanukkah is an especially happy holiday for children, with the giving of gelt, dreidels, and gifts. Jelly doughnuts, a favorite among children and grown-ups alike, have long been associated with Hanukkah.

Vanilla Crescent
Cookies

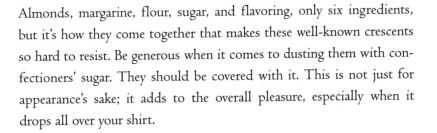

MAKES ABOUT 4½ DOZEN
COOKIES

Almonds, margarine, flour, sugar, and flavoring, only six ingredients, but it's how they come together that makes these well-known crescents so hard to resist. Be generous when it comes to dusting them with confectioners' sugar. They should be covered with it. This is not just for appearance's sake; it adds to the overall pleasure, especially when it drops all over your shirt.

½ pound (2 sticks) unsalted margarine
½ cup granulated vanilla sugar (see page 191)
2 teaspoons pure vanilla extract
2 cups all-purpose flour
¾ cup finely ground unblanched almonds
Confectioners' vanilla sugar (see page 191), for dusting

1. Preheat the oven to 350 degrees F. Line 2 large baking sheets with parchment paper.
2. In the bowl of an electric mixer fitted with the paddle attachment, cream the margarine on low speed just until fluffy. Add the granulated vanilla sugar and beat on low speed until combined. Beat in the vanilla. Scrape down the sides of the bowl with a rubber spatula and, still on low speed, gradually beat in the flour and the ground

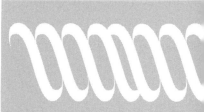

almonds until a dough comes together in a ball around the paddle, about 1 minute.

3. Shape the dough by scant teaspoonfuls into crescent shapes and arrange them on the prepared baking sheets, leaving 1½ inches in between. Bake 1 sheet at a time on the middle rack of the oven for 20 minutes, or just until the bottoms of the crescents are barely golden. Let cool for 5 minutes on the baking sheet, then transfer the cookies to a cooling rack to cool completely. Bake the remaining sheet of cookies and cool them in the same manner.

4. With a sifter or a fine-mesh sieve, dust the cooled cookies with the confectioners' vanilla sugar until nicely coated and snowy. Store in layers, separated by sheets of wax paper, in an airtight container.

Vanilla Sugar: You can make vanilla sugar with either granulated or confectioners' sugar. In a container with a tight-fitting lid, combine 1 cup sugar with a 1½-inch piece of vanilla bean. Cover and let stand, shaking the container every few days to redistribute the sugar, for at least 10 days to 2 weeks before using. Granulated vanilla sugar can be used in place of regular granulated sugar for baking and for dessert making to lend a hint of additional flavor.

Viennese Nut Cookies

MAKES ABOUT 3½ DOZEN
COOKIES

These European-style glazed walnut cookies have a hint of cinnamon, and are crispy on the edges and slightly soft within. Delicate and elegant, they look lovely on a serving platter.

½ pound (2 sticks) unsalted margarine
1 cup sugar
1 extra-large egg, beaten well
2¼ cups all-purpose flour
Egg wash of 1 egg white, beaten lightly
1 cup very finely chopped walnuts plus several
    tablespoons for sprinkling
Cinnamon sugar (page 183), for sprinkling

1. Preheat the oven to 350 degrees F. Line 2 large baking sheets with parchment paper.
2. In the bowl of a standing electric mixer fitted with the paddle attachment, cream the margarine with the sugar on medium speed until fluffy.
3. Add the egg and beat until incorporated. (The mixture will look curdled.)
4. Turn the machine to low and add the flour with the walnuts, beating until a dough forms around the paddle.

5. Scrape down the sides of the bowl, form the dough into a disk, wrap it in plastic wrap, and refrigerate it until firm enough to roll, at least I hour.

6. On a lightly floured surface, roll out the dough ¼ inch thick. With a 2-inch fluted cutter, cut out rounds and place them about I inch apart on the prepared baking sheets. Reroll the scraps and cut out more cookies in the same manner.

7. Brush the rounds lightly with the egg wash, sprinkle them with cinnamon sugar, and place a small dusting of the remaining chopped walnuts in the center of each.

8. Bake 10 to 12 minutes until the bottoms are just golden. Do not overbake. Remove the baking sheet to a wire rack and let the cookies cool for 5 minutes, then remove them to the rack to cool completely. Store, in layers, in an airtight container for up to 4 days.

Viennese Orange Cookies

Filled with the flavor of orange, this is another tender, short cookie that melts in your mouth. Rosette-shaped and delicate, these cookies are among the most elegant members of this collection. The chocolate-filled and -dipped variation tastes even richer.

14 tablespoons (1¾ sticks or 7 ounces) unsalted
  margarine
1 cup confectioners' sugar
2 tablespoons cornstarch
2 cups plus 1 tablespoon all-purpose flour
½ tablespoon pure vanilla extract
1 tablespoon finely grated orange zest

FILLING
8 tablespoons (1 stick) unsalted margarine
2 cups confectioners' sugar
¼ cup fresh orange juice
2 teaspoons freshly grated orange zest

Confectioners' sugar, for dusting

1. Preheat the oven to 350 degrees F. Line a large baking sheet with parchment paper.

2. In the bowl of a standing electric mixer fitted with the paddle attachment, cream the margarine and the confectioners' sugar on low speed until light and fluffy. Add the cornstarch and blend.

3. With the mixer still on low speed, add the flour, a little at a time, beating until incorporated. Mix in the vanilla and the orange zest.

4. Transfer the dough to a large pastry bag fitted with a 1 M (Wilton) star tip. Pipe rosettes of the dough, about 1 inch high by 1¼ inches wide, onto the baking sheet, leaving about 1 inch in between. (You will have 42 rosettes.) Bake for 14 minutes, or until just firm to the touch. Remove the baking sheet to a wire rack and let the cookies cool on the baking sheet.

5. Make the filling: Wash out the bowl of the mixer and the paddle and dry well. Fit the mixer with the paddle once again, add the margarine and the confectioners' sugar to the bowl, and cream on medium speed until light and fluffy. Add the orange juice and the zest and beat until well blended. Transfer the filling to a bowl, cover it with plastic wrap, and refrigerate it until firm enough to spread, about 30 minutes.

6. Assemble the cookies: With a metal spatula, spread the flat sides of half the cookies, 21 of them, with some of the orange filling. Press the remaining cookies, flat sides down, on the filling, making sandwich cookies. Arrange the cookies on a serving plate or cake plate and dust lightly with confectioners' sugar. Store in an airtight container in the refrigerator, where they will keep for up to 5 days. Bring to room temperature before serving.

VARIATION

Chocolate-Dipped Viennese Orange Cookies

Make the cookies as directed, but do not fill them with orange filling. While the cookies cool, in the top of a small double boiler melt 4 ounces bittersweet or semisweet chocolate, stirring, until shiny and smooth. Spread the flat sides of half of the cookies, 21 of them, with some of the melted chocolate, using it as filling. Make sandwiches with the remaining cookies. After assembling the cookies, dip them lightly, 1 at a time, into the still-warm chocolate, coating only half of the cookie. Hold the cookie over the pan for a second or two to let any excess chocolate drip back into the pan, then place it on a wire rack, taking care not to let the chocolate smudge. Let the cookies set at least 30 minutes in a cool place before serving or storing. Store, separated by layers of wax paper, in an airtight container in the refrigerator.

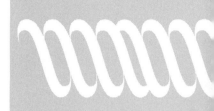

Chocolate Délices

If meringue appeals to you, then you must try these and the recipe for Pecan Délices that follows. The word *délice* means pleasure and happiness in French, which is just what these cookies inspire. And they are perfect for Passover.

2½ ounces bittersweet chocolate, chopped
⅓ cup egg whites, at room temperature (2 or 3 extra-large whites)
1½ cups sugar
1 cup finely ground unblanched almonds
1 teaspoon freshly grated lemon zest

1. Preheat the oven to 325 degrees F. Line 2 large baking sheets with parchment paper.
2. In the top of a small double boiler set over hot water, melt the chocolate, stirring, until smooth. Remove the pan from the heat and let it cool.
3. In the bowl of an electric mixer fitted with the whisk attachment, beat the egg whites on high speed until they hold soft peaks. Gradually add the sugar and beat until the meringue holds stiff peaks and is glossy.

4. With a rubber spatula, gently fold in the melted chocolate, ground almonds, and lemon zest until thoroughly combined. Do not overmix.

5. Drop the meringue mixture by heaping tablespoons onto the prepared baking sheets, leaving 2 inches in between each mound.

6. Bake 15 minutes. (The cookies will puff up slightly, then fall.) Transfer the baking sheet to a wire rack and let it cool. Do not try to remove the cookies before they are thoroughly cooled or they will break. Store, in layers separated by wax paper, in an airtight container for up to 4 days.

Pecan Délices

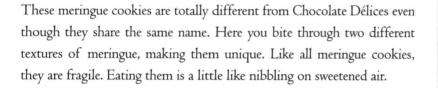

These meringue cookies are totally different from Chocolate Délices even though they share the same name. Here you bite through two different textures of meringue, making them unique. Like all meringue cookies, they are fragile. Eating them is a little like nibbling on sweetened air.

MAKES ABOUT 20 COOKIES, EACH 3 INCHES IN DIAMETER

4 extra-large egg whites, at room temperature
1½ cups sugar
1 cup coarsely ground pecans
1½ cups very finely ground (almost to a powder) pecans
2 teaspoons freshly grated lemon zest

1. Preheat the oven to 325 degrees F. Line 2 large baking sheets with parchment paper.

2. In the bowl of an electric mixer fitted with the whisk attachment, beat the egg whites on high speed until they hold stiff peaks. With the machine running, gradually add the sugar and beat until the meringue holds stiff peaks and is glossy.

3. Divide the meringue between 2 bowls. To one bowl—Bowl A—add the coarsely ground pecans and 1 teaspoon of the lemon zest, folding both in gently but thoroughly. To the other bowl of meringue—Bowl B—fold in the finely ground pecans and the remaining teaspoon of lemon zest.

4. Drop the meringue mixture in Bowl A by heaping tablespoons onto the prepared baking sheet, leaving 2 inches in between each mound. Now top each mound with a heaping tablespoon of the meringue in Bowl B.

5. Bake for 15 to 20 minutes until lightly colored and puffed. Transfer the baking sheets to cooling racks and let them cool. Do not try to transfer the cookies before they are thoroughly cooled or they may break. Store, in layers separated by wax paper, in an airtight container for up to 4 days.

ARE THEY STIFF YET?

The importance of properly beaten egg whites can never be overestimated when it comes to making meringue. Overbeat the whites and they turn grainy and unusable. Underbeat them and the meringue mixture literally has nowhere to go. The combination of air and heat is the driving force. Without sufficient air in a meringue, it will not rise.

To help you achieve perfect meringues, first address the ingredients and the technique itself. Be sure that the egg whites are at room temperature. The bowl and whisk of the electric mixer must be absolutely clean. The sugar you are adding should be measured out and ready to use in a dry-measure container.

Turn the mixer to high speed and beat the whites until they hold soft peaks. In this case, *soft* means slightly inflated, nothing more. Then, with the machine running, start adding the sugar gradually, pouring it in over the edge of the bowl. The whites, in turn, will gradually start to expand, increase in volume, and stiffen. Eventually they will stand in stiff peaks, so that when you drag the whisk through the mixture, the peaks will not fall over. At that point the meringue will also be white and glossy. Turn off the mixer. The meringue is ready.

That the meringue is ready is only part of the equation, though. If you are adding anything to the meringue, as in Chocolate or Pecan Délices, you need to fold the ingredients in gently. Do not stir them in vigorously or you risk deflating the meringue.

Passover
Baking

Passover Sponge Cake

Passover Chocolate Walnut Cake

Velvet Chocolate Cake

Chocolate Soufflé Roll

Success Cake

Oma's Hazelnut Torte

Chocolate Refrigerator Matzo Cake

Passover Fritters

Coconut Sandies

Lemon Shortbread Cookies

Hazelnut Cinnamon Cookies

Coconut Macaroons

Passover Brownies

Valentinos

Vanilla Meringues

Fresh Strawberry Sauce

Passover

Passover is an eight-day spring holiday commemorating the flight of the Jewish people from slavery in Egypt. Jews were forced to leave in such haste that their bread did not have time to rise. They put the loaves on their backs and let the sun bake them into hard, flat bread, called matzo. We eat matzo and other unleavened cakes on Passover to remind us of their flight. On the first two nights of the festival we have seders, where we read from the Haggadah, which recounts the Passover story. The service is followed by an elaborate multicourse meal.

Baking for Passover has been my greatest challenge as a professional baker. From my earliest childhood memories, I recall that no one was ever satisfied with the desserts that were served on Passover. My solution to the problem was to take recipes that were old favorites and adapt them to the dietary laws of the holiday. It meant testing and retesting. Matzo cake meal, nut flour, potato starch, and egg whites had to stand in for flour. My baker in the mid-1980s was Jackie Levy, and he was instrumental in helping me create my Passover repertoire. I can accurately say that the Passover desserts that follow are satisfying. In fact, I am frequently asked by customers who have sampled them over the holiday if they were really Kosher-for-Passover desserts.

Passover
Sponge Cake

MAKES ONE 10-INCH TUBE
CAKE, 8 TO 10 SERVINGS

On Passover there will typically be a selection of desserts at the holiday dinner, and almost assuredly there will be a sponge cake among them. This rendition is very traditional and light. In the absence of flour, well-beaten egg whites make the cake rise, so you might want to refer to page 200 for tips on how to whip them to maximum volume. Dust the cake with confectioners' sugar, if desired, or serve it with Fresh Strawberry Sauce (page 234).

> 6 extra-large eggs, separated, the whites at room
>   temperature
> 1¼ cups sugar
> Grated zest of 1 orange
> 1½ tablespoons fresh orange juice
> Grated zest of 1 lemon
> 1½ tablespoons fresh lemon juice
> ⅔ cup matzo cake meal
> ¼ teaspoon salt

1. Preheat the oven to 350 degrees F. Grease the bottom and sides of a 10-inch angel food cake pan.
2. In the bowl of a standing electric mixer fitted with the paddle attachment, beat the egg yolks on medium speed until lemon col-

ored. Gradually add the sugar and beat until thickened. Add the zest and juice of both the orange and lemon. Beat in the cake meal until incorporated. Transfer the mixture to a large bowl.

3. Wash out the bowl of the mixer well. Fit the mixer with the whisk attachment. Place the egg whites in the bowl, add the salt, and beat on high speed until the whites hold stiff but not dry peaks.

4. Stir one-quarter of the beaten whites into the cake base to lighten it. With a rubber spatula, fold the remaining whites in gently but thoroughly, mixing until no streaks of the beaten whites show.

5. Scrape the batter into the cake pan and smooth the top. Bake the cake for 50 minutes, or until a cake tester inserted in the center comes out clean. Transfer the cake to a wire rack to cool. To serve, unmold the cake from the pan and place it on a cake stand or plate.

Passover
Chocolate Walnut Cake

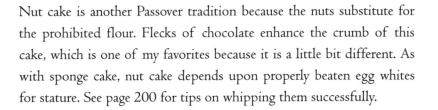

MAKES ONE 10-INCH TUBE
CAKE, 8 TO 10 SERVINGS

Nut cake is another Passover tradition because the nuts substitute for the prohibited flour. Flecks of chocolate enhance the crumb of this cake, which is one of my favorites because it is a little bit different. As with sponge cake, nut cake depends upon properly beaten egg whites for stature. See page 200 for tips on whipping them successfully.

> 1¼ cups finely ground walnuts
> ¾ cup very finely grated bittersweet chocolate
> 3 tablespoons matzo cake meal
> 1 dozen extra-large eggs, separated, the whites at
>   room temperature
> 1 cup granulated sugar
> 1 teaspoon finely grated lemon zest
> 1 teaspoon finely grated orange zest
> Confectioners' sugar, for sprinkling

1. Preheat the oven to 350 degrees F. Have ready a 10-inch angel food cake pan, but do not grease it.
2. In a large bowl, stir together the ground walnuts, ground chocolate, and cake meal.
3. In the bowl of a standing electric mixer fitted with the paddle attachment, beat the egg yolks on medium speed until lemon

colored. Gradually add the granulated sugar and beat until thickened. Add the lemon and orange zests and beat until incorporated.

4. Reduce the mixer speed to low and beat in the walnut-chocolate mixture until thoroughly combined. Transfer the mixture to a large bowl.

5. Wash out the mixer bowl well. Fit the mixer with the whisk attachment. Place the egg whites in the bowl and beat them on high speed until they stand in stiff but not dry peaks.

6. Stir one-quarter of the beaten whites into the walnut-chocolate base to lighten it. With a rubber spatula, fold in the remaining whites gently but thoroughly, mixing until no streaks of beaten whites show.

7. Pour the batter into the ungreased tube pan. Bake the cake for 1 hour and 10 minutes, or until the top springs back when tested. Transfer the cake to a wire rack to cool. Unmold the cake and place it on a cake stand or plate to serve. Before serving, sprinkle the top with confectioners' sugar. Store leftover cake, covered with plastic wrap, in the refrigerator for up to 4 days.

Velvet Chocolate Cake

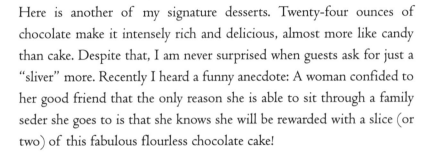

MAKES ONE 8-INCH CAKE, 12 TO 14 SERVINGS

Here is another of my signature desserts. Twenty-four ounces of chocolate make it intensely rich and delicious, almost more like candy than cake. Despite that, I am never surprised when guests ask for just a "sliver" more. Recently I heard a funny anecdote: A woman confided to her good friend that the only reason she is able to sit through a family seder she goes to is that she knows she will be rewarded with a slice (or two) of this fabulous flourless chocolate cake!

1½ pounds semisweet chocolate, chopped
15 tablespoons unsalted margarine, cut into chunks
1½ tablespoons instant coffee
8 extra-large eggs, separated, the whites at room temperature
1½ tablespoons granulated sugar
Confectioners' sugar for stenciling

1. Preheat the oven to 350 degrees F. Grease the bottom and sides of an 8-inch cake pan, 3 inches deep. Cut a round of parchment paper to fit the pan and line the pan with it.
2. In the top of a large double boiler set over hot water, melt the chocolate with the margarine and instant coffee, stirring, until

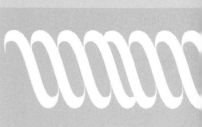

smooth and glossy. Remove the top of the boiler and let the mixture cool slightly.

3. Stir in the egg yolks, 1 at a time, beating well after each addition.

4. In the bowl of a standing electric mixer fitted with the whisk attachment, beat the egg whites on high speed to soft peaks. Gradually add the granulated sugar and beat until the whites stand in stiff but not dry peaks.

5. With a rubber spatula, stir about one-quarter of the whites into the chocolate base to lighten it. Fold the remaining whites in gently but thoroughly, mixing until no streaks of beaten whites show.

6. Pour the batter into the pan. Place the cake pan in a larger baking pan and pour hot water to come halfway up the sides of the cake pan. Carefully transfer the pans to the oven and bake the cake for 35 to 40 minutes (the top of the cake in the center will just be set). Remove the baking pan from the oven, remove the cake pan from the water bath, and let it cool completely on a wire rack at room temperature. Transfer the cake in the pan to the refrigerator and chill ovenight or until serving time.

7. Unmold the chilled cake, remove the paper liner, and invert the cake right side up. Do not try to unmold the cake before it is fully chilled or it will break. Place a decorative stencil on top of the cake and dust confectioners' sugar through a fine-meshed sieve over the top. Carefully remove the stencil.

8. Serve the cake in slices. Some people love it with fresh raspberries as a garnish. (The cake can also be served at room temperature, although it will be softer.) The cake keeps, covered with plastic wrap, in the refrigerator for up to 3 days.

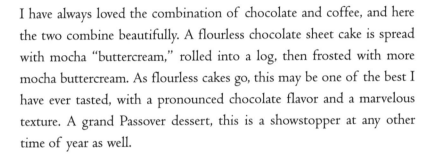

Chocolate Soufflé Roll

I have always loved the combination of chocolate and coffee, and here the two combine beautifully. A flourless chocolate sheet cake is spread with mocha "buttercream," rolled into a log, then frosted with more mocha buttercream. As flourless cakes go, this may be one of the best I have ever tasted, with a pronounced chocolate flavor and a marvelous texture. A grand Passover dessert, this is a showstopper at any other time of year as well.

> 8 ounces semisweet chocolate, chopped
> 4 tablespoons espresso or strong coffee
> 7 extra-large eggs, separated, the whites at room
>   temperature
> ¾ cup sugar
> Unsweetened cocoa powder, for dusting on the cake
> 1 recipe Mocha "Buttercream" (page 92)

1. Preheat the oven to 350 degrees F. Grease a 15 × 10-inch jelly-roll pan. Line the pan with parchment paper and grease the paper.
2. In the top of a double boiler set over hot water, melt the chocolate with the espresso, stirring, until shiny and smooth. Remove the top of the double boiler and let the mixture cool slightly.

3. In the bowl of a standing electric mixer fitted with the paddle attachment, beat the egg yolks with ½ cup of the sugar until thick and lemon colored. Scrape the slightly cooled chocolate mixture into the yolk mixture and combine well.

4. Beat the egg whites with a handheld mixer until foamy. Gradually add the remaining ¼ cup sugar and beat until stiff but not dry peaks form. With a rubber spatula, fold the beaten whites in the chocolate cake base, mixing until no streaks of beaten whites show.

5. Spread the batter in an even layer over the prepared pan and bake the sheet cake for 20 minutes.

6. Remove the pan from the oven and immediately place a dampened clean kitchen towel over the sheet cake. Let cool completely at room temperature.

7. To assemble the roll: Remove the kitchen towel and dust the top of the sheet cake lightly with cocoa powder. Place a large piece of parchment paper on the work surface and invert the sheet cake onto it. Remove the piece of parchment on the top.

8. With a long-bladed metal spatula, spread about 1½ cups of the mocha buttercream over the surface of the cake. Using the paper as an aid to roll up the sheet cake and starting with the long side nearest you, roll the cake into a long, relatively tight cylinder. (Do not exert too much pressure when you roll because the cake may break or the buttercream will ooze out.) When you have finished rolling the log, place it, seam side down, on a baking sheet and refrigerate it, wrapped in parchment paper, until firm.

9. To serve, remove the parchment paper. With a serrated knife, trim the uneven, crusty ends of the log. With the spatula, frost the roll with the remaining mocha buttercream, starting with the top and covering the sides and ends evenly. With 2 long spatulas, carefully transfer the cake roll to a long cake platter. Serve. Store the cake, its cut end covered with plastic wrap, in the refrigerator for up to 3 days.

Success Cake

MAKES ONE 3-LAYER, 10-INCH
CAKE, 10 TO 12 SERVINGS

This gorgeous-looking cake is really a *dacquoise*, France's one-of-a-kind meringue-and-buttercream creation. Elegant and special, it is surprisingly light and lends itself to customizing on the part of the baker. You can use only one "buttercream" for the filling and frosting, or you can use three different kinds, like vanilla, chocolate, and mocha. You can also fill it with Chocolate Mousse (page 98), reserving the buttercream for the frosting only. If you like your meringue crunchy, assemble it not too long before serving. (You can, of course, make the individual components ahead.) If you prefer meringue that is slightly softened and chewy, prepare the cake the day before the holiday.

2¼ cups ground toasted blanched or unblanched
    almonds
1 tablespoon potato starch
6 extra-large egg whites, at room temperature
1½ cups granulated sugar
3 cups "buttercream" of choice (pages 90–93), for
    filling and frosting the cake
1 cup slivered almonds, toasted, for sprinkling
Confectioners' sugar, for dusting

I. Preheat the oven to 200 degrees F. Have ready 2 large baking sheets and 2 sheets of parchment paper cut to fit the baking sheets.

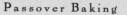

2. With a pencil, trace the circumference of a 10-inch cake pan 2 times on one of the sheets of parchment, pressing down firmly. On the remaining sheet of parchment, trace the pan 1 time. Turn each parchment sheet over and place, penciled side down, on one of the baking sheets. Make sure that you are able to see the pan outlines on each of the sheets.

3. Onto a sheet of wax paper, sift together the almonds and the potato starch.

4. In the bowl of a standing electric mixer fitted with the whisk attachment, beat the egg whites on medium speed until foamy. Increase the speed to high and gradually start adding the sugar, beating until the meringue is glossy and holds peaks.

5. With a rubber spatula, fold in the ground almond mixture gently but thoroughly.

6. Scoop the meringue mixture into a large pastry bag fitted with a large plain tip. Starting from the outside edge of the outline, pipe meringue in concentric circles until the 10-inch outline is filled. Make rounds of meringue on the remaining 2 outlines in the same manner.

7. Bake the meringues for 1 hour and 15 minutes. The meringues will be lightly tan in color. Remove and let cool on the baking sheets.

8. When ready to assemble the cake, place 1 meringue layer on a large serving plate and spread buttercream in an even layer over it. Top with another meringue and spread it with buttercream. Make a top layer in the same manner, then cover the sides of the cake with the remaining buttercream. Scatter the slivered almonds over the top and sides and dust with confectioners' sugar. Serve. Depending upon how you like the texture of your meringue—crunchy and crisp or softened and chewy—the cake can be stored, loosely covered with plastic wrap, in the refrigerator for 1 day.

Oma's Hazelnut Torte

MAKES ONE 8-INCH CAKE, 8 TO
10 SERVINGS

Here is the quintessential Passover nut cake, the one I remember from my childhood. *Oma* means grandmother in German, and while Grandma Leah never passed her recipe along to me, this is very close to the one she would make for the family on Passover year after year. The hazelnuts made it special then, and now.

> 5 extra-large eggs, separated, the whites at room
>   temperature
> ½ cup sugar
> 1 cup hazelnuts, toasted and skinned (page 173),
>   very finely ground
> ¼ cup matzo cake meal
> Pinch of salt

1. Preheat the oven to 375 degrees F. Grease an 8-inch cake pan.
2. In the bowl of a standing electric mixer fitted with the paddle attachment, beat the egg yolks and sugar on medium speed until triple in volume, about 5 to 7 minutes. Fold in the hazelnuts and the cake meal until fully incorporated.
3. Place the egg whites and the salt in a large bowl. With a handheld electric mixer, beat the whites on high speed until they hold stiff but

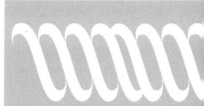

not dry peaks. Stir one-quarter of the beaten whites into the yolk mixture to lighten it, then with a rubber spatula gently fold in the remaining whites until no streaks of white show.

4. Scrape the batter lightly into the cake pan and level the top. Bake the cake for 30 to 40 minutes until a cake tester inserted in the center comes out clean. Transfer the pan to a wire rack and let cool for 5 minutes. Unmold the cake, turn it right side up, and let it cool completely on the rack. To serve, place the cake on a cake plate or stand. Store leftover cake, covered with plastic wrap, in the refrigerator for the length of the holiday.

Chocolate Refrigerator Matzo Cake

MAKES ABOUT 8 SERVINGS

During Passover, there is a certain challenge in using matzo in as many creative ways as possible. Here is one clever way my friend, literary agent, and mother of three, Carla Glasser, suggested. Children especially like this, Carla explains, because it is slightly different and has chocolate in it! She's absolutely right on both counts. It is also so easy to make you could do it with the children, one day in advance of serving, if you like.

12 tablespoons (1½ sticks) unsalted margarine

¾ cup sugar

2 extra-large eggs, separated, the whites at room temperature

¼ cup unsweetened cocoa powder, sifted

Pinch of salt

6 whole matzos

1 cup Orange-Scented Sugar Syrup (page 94)

Grated semisweet chocolate, for garnish

I. In the bowl of a standing electric mixer fitted with the paddle attachment, cream the margarine and sugar on medium speed until fluffy. Add the egg yolks and cocoa and beat until blended.

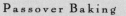

2. Place the egg whites and the salt in a bowl. Beat with a handheld electric mixer on medium-high speed until they hold stiff peaks. Fold the beaten egg whites into the cocoa mixture until no streaks of white show.

3. Brush both sides of one of the matzos with some of the orange sugar syrup and place on a large flat serving plate. Spread an even layer of the cocoa mixture over the matzo. Continue to make layers with the remaining matzos, brushing each first with the sugar syrup and then spreading them with the cocoa mixture in the same manner. Spread the remaining cocoa mixture around the sides as a frosting and sprinkle the grated chocolate over the top. Chill until 30 minutes before serving. Store leftover cake, covered with plastic wrap, in the refrigerator for 2 days.

Passover Fritters

When we lived in Bayside, my neighbor Trudy, who came from Germany, used to make the most delicious Passover fritters, and this is my interpretation of how I think she prepared them. Trudy always served them for dessert, but you can also offer them at breakfast as an alternative to matzo *brei*. They are at their absolute best eaten as soon as they are made—while they are still warm. Get some helpers in the kitchen, fry up a batch, roll the fritters generously in the cinnamon sugar, and enjoy.

> 4 whole matzos
> 2 cups Orange-Scented Sugar Syrup (page 94)
> 3 extra-large eggs, beaten lightly
> 1 cup dark raisins
> ¼ cup ground blanched almonds
> 1 cup matzo cake meal
> Grated zest of 2 lemons, or less, to taste
> 1 cup sugar
> 2 teaspoons ground cinnamon
> 1 quart Kosher-for-Passover oil for deep frying

1. Break the matzos into a large bowl and pour the orange sugar syrup over them. Let stand 10 to 15 minutes, or until the matzos have absorbed the sugar syrup.

2. Add the eggs to the softened matzo mixture and stir well to combine. Stir in the raisins, almonds, cake meal, and lemon zest, mixing until well blended. Using a ¼-cup measure, shape the mixture into balls.

3. Meanwhile, in a large, deep, heavy-bottomed skillet or saucepan, heat the oil to 250 degrees F on a deep-fry thermometer. Carefully add the fritters, 4 or 5 at a time, to the hot oil and deep-fry them, turning them as needed until golden brown all over, 5 to 7 minutes. With a skimmer, transfer the fritters to paper towels to drain. Let the oil reheat to 250 degrees F on the thermometer and deep-fry the remaining balls, letting them drain in the same manner.

4. On a large sheet of wax paper, stir together the sugar and cinnamon until well combined. While the fritters are still warm, roll them in the cinnamon sugar until well coated. Place the fritters on a serving plate and serve at once.

Coconut
Sandies

MAKES 30 TO 35 COOKIES

These sweet crumbly cookies are reminiscent of those you might make throughout the year, only they are made with matzo cake meal. Even though they contain coconut, they are completely different from Coconut Macaroons (page 226), and there is no reason why you can't serve both at the Passover seder.

> 1½ cups sugar
> 3¼ cups very finely flaked desiccated coconut
> 8 tablespoons (1 stick) unsalted margarine
> 1 extra-large egg
> ¾ cup matzo cake meal
> Finely grated zest of 1 lemon
> Juice of ½ lemon

1. Preheat the oven to 350 degrees F. Grease a large cookie sheet.
2. In a bowl combine 1 cup each of the sugar and coconut; spread in an even layer on a piece of parchment paper.
3. In the bowl of a standing electric mixer fitted with the paddle attachment, cream the margarine and the remaining ½ cup sugar on medium speed until fluffy. Add the egg and beat until incorporated. Beat in the cake meal, the remaining 2¼ cups coconut, and the lemon zest and juice until combined.

4. Shape the batter into balls, each about the size of a half-dollar. Roll the balls, 1 at a time, in the coconut-sugar mixture, coating completely. Place on the cookie sheet, leaving about 2 inches in between. With the back of a fork, make a crosshatch pattern on the top of each cookie, pressing down on the top to flatten the cookies slightly.

5. Bake for 20 to 25 minutes until the cookies are golden brown. With a metal spatula, transfer the cookies to a wire rack to cool. Store, in even layers, in an airtight container for 1 week.

Lemon Shortbread Cookies

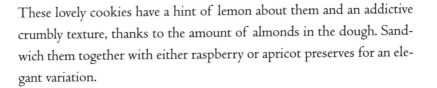

These lovely cookies have a hint of lemon about them and an addictive crumbly texture, thanks to the amount of almonds in the dough. Sandwich them together with either raspberry or apricot preserves for an elegant variation.

> 1 cup finely ground blanched almonds
> ¾ cup matzo cake meal
> ½ cup potato starch
> ⅛ teaspoon ground nutmeg
> 8 tablespoons (1 stick) unsalted margarine
> ½ cup sugar
> 1 extra-large egg
> Grated zest and juice of 1 large lemon

1. Preheat the oven to 350 degrees F. Line a large baking sheet with parchment paper.
2. In a bowl stir together the almonds, cake meal, potato starch, and nutmeg.
3. In the bowl of a standing electric mixer fitted with the paddle attachment, cream the margarine and sugar on medium speed until fluffy. Scrape down the sides of the bowl with a rubber spatula. Add the egg and lemon zest and juice and beat until incorporated.

4. Reduce the mixer speed to low, add the dry ingredients, and beat until a dough forms.

5. Shape the dough, 1 rounded teaspoon at a time, into balls and place them about 1 inch apart on the lined baking sheet. Press each mound with the back of a fork until it is about ½ inch thick, then press again in the opposite direction to make a crosshatch pattern. Bake for 20 to 25 minutes until golden brown. With a metal spatula, transfer the cookies to a wire rack to cool. Store in an airtight container for up to 1 week.

Hazelnut Cinnamon Cookies

What I love about these meringue-based nut cookies is that they are different in both shape and texture from what is expected on the Passover table. And, if you toast and skin the hazelnuts ahead of time, they are simple to make. Given the amount of effort involved in preparing a seder or two, an easy recipe is welcome!

3 extra-large egg whites, at room temperature
½ cup granulated sugar
2 cups ground toasted and skinned hazelnuts
    (see page 173)
1 tablespoon ground cinnamon
1 cup confectioners' sugar, for rolling

1. Preheat the oven to 400 degrees F. Grease a large baking sheet.
2. In the bowl of a standing electric mixer fitted with the whisk attachment, beat the egg whites until foamy. With the machine running, gradually add ¼ cup of the granulated sugar and beat on high speed until the whites hold stiff peaks.
3. With a rubber spatula, fold in the remaining ¼ cup granulated sugar, hazelnuts, and cinnamon until combined.

4. Shape the batter into small balls, about 1 inch in diameter, and place 2 inches apart on the baking sheet. Bake 10 to 15 minutes until just firm to the touch.

5. While the cookies are baking, spread the confectioners' sugar on a piece of parchment paper.

6. Remove the cookies from the oven and, while they are still hot, roll them in the confectioners' sugar to coat. Let cool. Store, in layers, in an airtight container for up to 3 days.

Coconut Macaroons

MAKES ABOUT 3 DOZEN
MACAROONS

I bet you have never tasted macaroons this good. When my French-Moroccan baker first made these in Great Neck in 1985, I almost swooned. Then he suggested dipping them in melted semisweet chocolate. These macaroons or the chocolate-coated variation are a treat you must try at least once in your life. For directions on how to dip the macaroons, see the end of this recipe.

A final thought on undipped macaroons: Consider using them in trifle, where they lend wonderful flavor and texture.

5½ cups very finely flaked desiccated coconut
Finely grated zest and juice of 1 large lemon
6 extra-large egg whites
2¼ cups sugar

1. Preheat the oven to 350 degrees F. Line a large baking sheet with parchment paper.
2. In a large bowl, stir together the coconut and lemon zest until well combined.
3. In a large saucepan, combine the egg whites and sugar over medium-high heat, stirring constantly, until the sugar melts and the mixture turns almost marshmallow-white in color. Stir in the coconut. Stirring constantly, combine the mixture well. Add the lemon juice and

continue to stir until incorporated. (The mixture will be sticky and come together in a mass.)

4. Carefully spoon the batter into a large pastry bag fitted with a #9 star tip and pipe mounds, each about 2 inches wide and 1½ inches high, onto the prepared baking sheet, leaving ¾ inch in between. (You should have 36 mounds when done.) If you don't have a pastry bag, use a tablespoon to spoon mounds of the batter onto the baking sheet.

5. Bake for about 10 minutes, or until the macaroons are lightly golden on the top and the edges of the mounds slightly darker. Remove the baking sheet from the oven and let the cookies cool on the sheet. Store the macaroons, in layers, in an airtight container for 1 week.

V A R I A T I O N

Chocolate-Covered Coconut Macaroons

In the top of a double boiler set over hot water, melt 6 ounces chopped semisweet chocolate, stirring, until glossy. Dip the cooled macaroons, 1 at a time, into the chocolate, covering them completely. Hold the cookie over the pan to let the excess chocolate drip back in. Place the cookies on a wire rack set over a baking sheet lined with parchment paper and let set for at least 30 minutes, depending upon the temperature. Store in layers, separated by wax paper, in the refrigerator.

Passover
Brownies

ℰ

MAKES 16 SQUARES,
EACH 2¼ INCHES SQUARE

While many Passover desserts are for the grown-ups, here is one specif-ically for the children. Be careful not to overbake these brownies. They are at their best when fudgy.

8 ounces bittersweet chocolate, chopped
8 tablespoons (1 stick) unsalted margarine
4 extra-large eggs
1⅓ cups sugar
1 cup matzo cake meal
¼ teaspoon salt
½ cup miniature bittersweet chocolate chips

1. Preheat the oven to 350 degrees F. Grease a 9-inch square baking pan.
2. In the top of a double boiler set over hot water, melt the chocolate with the margarine, stirring, until glossy and combined. Remove the pan from the water. Let cool slightly.
3. In the bowl of a standing electric mixer fitted with the paddle attachment, beat the eggs with the sugar on medium speed until lemon colored. Add the melted chocolate mixture and beat until combined. On low speed beat in the cake meal and salt. Stir in the chocolate chips until evenly distributed.

4. Spread the batter in the prepared pan, leveling the top with a spatula, and bake for 18 to 20 minutes for moist and fudgy-in-the-middle brownies. Lengthen the baking time by no more than 3 to 4 minutes for cakelike brownies. Remove the pan to a cooling rack and let cool before cutting into squares or bars. Store leftovers, covered with plastic wrap, in the refrigerator for 3 or 4 days.

Valentinos

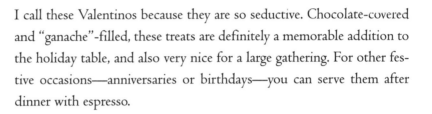

MAKES ABOUT 3 DOZEN
CONFECTIONS

I call these Valentinos because they are so seductive. Chocolate-covered and "ganache"-filled, these treats are definitely a memorable addition to the holiday table, and also very nice for a large gathering. For other festive occasions—anniversaries or birthdays—you can serve them after dinner with espresso.

> **12 ounces almond paste (do not use marzipan)**
> **4 ounces sugar**
> **2 extra-large egg whites**
> **Dr. Paul's "Ganache" (page 100), for the filling**
> **Melted semisweet chocolate, still warm, for dipping**

1. Preheat the oven to 350 degrees F. Line a baking sheet with parchment paper.
2. Crumble the almond paste into the bowl of a standing electric mixer, breaking it up into small pieces; fit the mixer with the paddle attachment and add the sugar and egg whites. Combine the mixture on low speed until the almond paste is pulverized and the mixture is smooth. Transfer the mixture to a small pastry bag fitted with a plain small tip.
3. Pipe the almond paste mixture into rounds, each about the size of a quarter, onto the lined baking sheet, leaving about 1 inch in between. Bake the rounds for 10 to 12 minutes until very lightly golden but not dry. Remove the baking sheet to a cooling rack and let cool.

4. To assemble the confections: Take a level tablespoon of the ganache and mound it on top of each of the rounds, rounding it off with a spatula to even the sides.

5. Make sure that the melted chocolate has cooled enough to touch, but is still warm. Take the confections, 1 at a time, and dip them upside down into the melted chocolate, coating each completely and letting the excess drip back into the pan. Place the dipped confection back on the baking sheet. When all the confections have been dipped, place the baking sheet in the refrigerator to set the chocolate. To serve, arrange the confections on a serving plate and let them stand briefly at room temperature before serving. Store, in a single layer, in an airtight container in the refrigerator for 3 to 4 days.

Vanilla Meringues

Makes 10 to 12 meringues,
each 1½ to 2 inches wide

Meringues are a true Passover staple, and these are out-of-this-world delicious, perfect for a holiday table. You don't even need a pastry bag to make them because I much prefer the look of free-form meringues. The chocolate variation requires only the addition of cocoa powder to the egg white mixture, so it is easy to offer two different types at the same time.

Because they are low in fat but satisfyingly sweet, meringues are very nice to serve year-round, especially with fresh fruit desserts. They also keep beautifully. And on the occasion when you are serving a dairy meal and calorie count is not a consideration, serve them Argentina style—sandwiched together with whipped cream.

3 extra-large egg whites, at room temperature
¾ cup sugar
1 teaspoon pure vanilla extract

1. Preheat the oven to 250 degrees F. Grease and flour a large baking sheet.
2. In the bowl of an electric mixer fitted with the whisk attachment, beat the egg whites until they hold soft peaks. Gradually add the sugar, 1 tablespoon at a time. Add the vanilla and beat until the meringue holds stiff peaks and is glossy.

232

3. Using 2 tablespoons, drop the mixture off one spoon, pushing it with the second spoon, onto the prepared baking sheet; leave 2 inches in between the mounds.

4. Bake for 1 hour. Remove the baking sheet to a cooling rack and let cool. Store, in a single layer, in an airtight container for several days.

VARIATIONS

Chocolate Meringues

Make the meringue mixture as directed in the recipe, and after beating in the vanilla, add 2 tablespoons unsweetened cocoa powder; beat until fully incorporated. Finish the meringues as directed in Steps 2 and 3.

Tinted Meringues

There is a fun restaurant on East Sixtieth Street in Manhattan called Serendipity 3. Back in the mid-eighties, we delivered meringues to them, and I will never forget the day they placed an order for pink meringues. The fellows at Serendipity were way ahead of the curve, as I have noticed that tinted meringues—pink, yellow, green—seem to be in vogue now, some fifteen years later. If you want to make colored meringues, add a tiny drop of liquid food coloring to the meringue mixture. Know that even a little food coloring goes a long way.

Fresh Strawberry Sauce

Makes about 2 cups

1 pint strawberries, hulled and sliced
¾ cup sugar
¾ cup water
1 tablespoon fresh lemon juice
¼ teaspoon ground cinnamon

In a saucepan combine all the ingredients and cook over medium heat, stirring, for about 30 minutes until reduced and thickened to the consistency of a puree. Remove the pan from the heat, transfer the sauce to a bowl, and cool it to room temperature. Cover the sauce and chill it well, for several hours at least, before serving. The sauce keeps, covered with plastic wrap, in the refrigerator for 3 days.

A Good Solution

Passover sponge cake can look quite plain. Its appearance doesn't make it any less tasty—just unadorned. If you want to add color and flavor in an easy way, try this fresh strawberry sauce, which also happens to be good served with made-with-flour cakes, white or chocolate, at other times of the year. The touch of cinnamon makes the sauce taste as if it had been made with *fraises des bois*, wild strawberries.

Index